Mrs. Oliphant

Memoir of Count de Montalembert

A Chapter of recent french History - Vol. I

Mrs. Oliphant

Memoir of Count de Montalembert
A Chapter of recent french History - Vol. I

ISBN/EAN: 9783337073923

Printed in Europe, USA, Canada, Australia, Japan

Cover: Foto ©ninafisch / pixelio.de

More available books at **www.hansebooks.com**

MEMOIR

OF

COUNT DE MONTALEMBERT

PEER OF FRANCE

DEPUTY FOR THE DEPARTMENT OF DOUBS

A CHAPTER OF RECENT FRENCH HISTORY

BY

MRS OLIPHANT

AUTHOR OF THE 'LIFE OF EDWARD IRVING,'
'S. FRANCIS OF ASSISI,' ETC.

IN TWO VOLUMES

VOL. I.

WILLIAM BLACKWOOD AND SONS
EDINBURGH AND LONDON
MDCCCLXXII

The Right of Translation is reserved

TO THE COMPANION OF HIS LIFE

THE GUARDIAN OF HIS MEMORY

ANNA, COMTESSE DE MONTALEMBERT

(NÉE COMTESSE DE MERODE)

This Book is Inscribed

WITH AFFECTIONATE SYMPATHY AND REGARD

PREFACE.

My first duty in sending this book into the world is to acknowledge the extreme and most generous confidence and kindness with which the family of the Count de Montalembert have honoured me. Both in her own hospitable home at La Roche, and in mine, the Comtesse de Montalembert, with the grace which belongs to her name, has afforded me every possible opportunity of increasing my acquaintance with the character and sentiments of her noble and distinguished husband; and no words can be strong enough to express my obligations to her. Everything in these volumes which concerns the youth and private life of Count de Montalembert has thus been drawn direct from the fountain-head.

So far, however, as concerns his public life, I have taken advantage chiefly of his own exposition of himself which is to be found in his published works. And as it was inevitable that Madame de Montalembert, a most sincere and fervent Catholic, should differ from my conclusions and sentiments in various important particulars, I am anxious to exonerate her entirely from all responsibility in a work, which is written from a point of view very different from hers — which cannot be expected to be in accordance with her religious belief—and in which there are many feelings and expressions, on this subject, with which she can have no sympathy. Lest her great kindness to me should entangle her in a supposed assent to any of my political or religious opinions, I feel it my duty to state most distinctly that this has not been the case ; and that while receiving with gratitude the kind communications made to me, I have reserved my own opinion on all points—the only possible means by which an artist, of whatever description, can hope to produce a genuine and recognisable portrait.

This statement is perhaps unnecessary for the English reader; but if I am so fortunate as to obtain any readers in France, they will better understand its propriety. Having said this, I repeat my sincere and cordial acknowledgments to Madame de Montalembert and her daughters; to M. le Vicomte de Meaux, the son-in-law and executor of Count de Montalembert; to M. Theophile Foisset, and M. Cornudet, his life-long friends; to the Right Honourable W. Monsell, through whose kind intervention several letters have been intrusted to me; and to Mrs Craven, the accomplished authoress of 'Le Recit d'une Sœur.'

M. O. W. OLIPHANT.

WINDSOR, 1872.

CONTENTS OF THE FIRST VOLUME.

MEMOIR

OF

COUNT DE MONTALEMBERT.

CHAPTER I.

HIS EARLY YEARS.

CHARLES FORBES RENÉ DE MONTALEMBERT, son of a noble French *émigré* and his English wife, was born in London on the 15th May 1810. The two races which culminated in this one figure, the most illustrious which has distinguished either line, communicated to him so completely their double character, that it is interesting to note their characteristics from the beginning. The house of Montalembert was the most distinguished of the two, though not older perhaps than that of the Forbes, who can be traced back into the legendary twilight of Scottish history.   The Montalemberts had their origin in Poitou.   They were a warlike and chivalrous race, soldiers from their earliest appearance in history.   Among the brief records inscribed beside their shields in the family tree by the affectionate hand of their descendant, there are scarcely more than half-a-dozen who are not marked as *tué* in some war or feud of their time   A seigneur of the name, Montalembert d'Essé, appears by the side of the most chivalrous of French kings, Francis I., as described by his royal brother-in-arms.   "Here are four of us, gentlemen of la Guyenne," says Francis, "I, Sanzac, Montalembert, and la Chasteigneraye, ready to encounter all comers in France."   Of this same Montalembert, when appointed first gentleman of the royal bed-chamber, the courtiers said that he was more fit to charge the enemy than to dress the king— "Plus propre à donner une camisade à l'ennemi qu'une chemise au roi."   At an earlier period, a crusading knight had inscribed upon the shield of the family the cross, most fit cognisance of their last descendant; and later, the line produced, in the person of Marc-René, Marquis de Montalembert, a name which holds its place by that of Vauban in the history of scientific warfare.   The brother of this great engineer was the grandfather of Charles de Montalembert. He was one of the nobles driven out of France by the Revolution—a man whose beautiful melancholy face, full of that sense of failure and tragic sadness which would seem the most natural mood of a man of his class at that terrible period, stands out in the quaintest strangest contrast with the thoughtful but comfortable and well-to-do countenance of the grandfather Forbes, his contemporary, whose share in the existence of the young Charles was still greater than his. They are types of different worlds, as well as different races. The cycle of chivalry, of romance, of poetic elevation over the common cares and needs of rude existence, shows in the one—at its end, consciously dying out, with all the grace of misfortune not personally deserved, that mournful beauty of loss and sacrifice which softens the world towards a fallen cause, howsoever that cause may have deserved its fall. Thus stands Jean de Montalembert at one side of the portal ; and on the other James Forbes, with trim peruke and calm countenance, strong in English order, prosperity, and progress, expecting nothing but good, hearing of nothing but victory, raises with cheerful confidence the curtain of life for the new actor about to step upon that tragic stage

No young beginner could have had predecessors more perfect in their typical character; no new soul could have more perfectly embodied in one those two great currents of the past.

It is, however, with his grandfather Forbes that the early life of the young Montalembert is most closely connected.   It is not necessary for our purpose to establish what was the exact line of connection with the Irish Earls of Granard, which is one of the distinctions of the family; but it is apparent that they did not spring from any of the better known Scotch branches of the name, as has been generally supposed.   James Forbes himself was an Englishman by birth and breeding.   He was born of that class of English gentry which then sent its sons in shoals to India, with all the more comfort and confidence that in those days interest ruled supreme, and competitive examinations had not been thought of.   He went out to Bombay as a writer, and was twenty years in India and the East.   He was the author of several books, one of which, 'Oriental Memoirs,' is still known, and procured for him a considerable reputation in the scientific as well as in the literary world.   He was a great traveller, a minute observer, fond of natural science, and as learned in it as that early epoch of scientific investigation permitted—an excellent draughtsman, and most painstaking collector. Though the ordinary reader is no longer familiar with his name, he had acquired sufficient reputation among his contemporaries to be specially released by Napoleon as an English *savant*—on the intercession of Carnot, then head of the French Institute, and Sir Joseph Banks, the President of the Royal Society—after a short imprisonment at Verdun, among the other *détenus* seized and held fast after the short peace of 1803. About five years after this adventure his only child married the young *émigré*, Marc-René de Montalembert, son of Count Jean, who had been brought to England by the first emigration at the age of fifteen, and had taken service with the English army in India. Mr Forbes was at this time residing in a pretty house at Stanmore, near Harrow, where he had settled on his return from India; but it was apparently in his house in Albemarle Street that the little Charles, his first grandchild, the heir of both races, was born.

At a very early age, fifteen months, the child was given over entirely to his grandfather's keeping; for these were stirring days for all connected with the emigration, and change was rife and hope high. The young Count de Montalembert and his wife were moving hither and thither as a soldier's household must, and in 1814 went back to France with the restored Bourbons; so that the arrangement which secured a peaceful home and up-bringing for their little boy was no doubt a relief to their anxieties, as well as a most blessed consolation to the old man left behind. The child thus given to Mr Forbes in his old age seems to have become at once the object of that adoring love, a sentiment at once more tender and more absorbing than simple paternity, which so often, passing over the head of one generation, links age and infancy together in the most beautiful of connections. The well-filled library at Stanmore became at once the scene of one of the most touching little dramas of domestic affection. There were but two actors in it; and, as usual in all the deepest of human sentiments, one only was active, the other passive. The old man among his books, with all the treasures of his well-spent life around him, woke up in the stillness of his solitude at sight of the bright-eyed baby in the corner, trained to play quietly, lest it should disturb him, and lifting wondering blue eyes from time to time to the tranquil aged figure which filled up its little world. The grandfather was stirred into a tender enthusiasm by the presence of the child for whom his own many experiences, his information, his varied acquirements, might form an inheritance as real, and perhaps not less important, than his worldly possessions. It was not as a *fils des croisés*, the scion of a chivalrous and warlike race, and one of the natural leaders in the future of a distracted and unhappy country, that this good, learned, respectable, and pious Englishman regarded his little grandson; but as his own boy, heir of all his thoughts and studies, a little creature to be trained into the same habits of investigation and thoughtful inquiry which were dear to himself. The thought that thus all his own labours might fructify and bless the world after him, turned into delight and eagerness, with Mr Forbes, those struggles of the old and solitary to keep themselves occupied and cheerful which are often so pathetic to spectators. To him was given the privilege of making his own life, and its studies and knowledge the foundation of a new life of infinite capability and hope.

He set to work at once upon this delightful enterprise. He would almost seem to have thought of nothing else from the moment of the child's birth. The great work of his life, that from which he had hoped to win the

gentle recollection of posterity, a thought
sweet to all men, his 'Oriental Memoirs,' became the tangible centre of all these loving
thoughts and anxious labours. The work itself
is chiefly upon the natural history of the East.
He took its little kernel of printed matter, which
was for all the world, and enshrined it in a
succession of immense volumes, full of illustrations done by his own and other hands. Before little Charles was able to utter an articulate
syllable, this great work was begun. With pen
and pencil, both of which he could use skilfully,
with the artist's brush, and even with the more
homely collector's paste and scissors, the fond
grandfather laboured year after year, as his
little boy grew. Leisure, learned and tranquil
and tender, is visible in every page; the very
handwriting is a wonder—love and patience are
in every stroke. He wrote fond letters to the
baby, to serve as prefaces to his vast work. He
placed a portrait of the little face he loved so
well, drawn by his own hand, with pretty gar-
lands of grandfatherly verse, as the frontispiece:
to these he added portraits, also by himself, of
his own family—portraits which he had taken
with him when he went a boy to India, but
which now, like every other precious thing he
possessed, were to swell the inheritance of this

little heir of his soul. Never was a more wonderful monument of an old man's love. The spectator gazes at the baby portrait looking at him with round blue eyes out of the ample page, with that faltering laugh which has tears in it. This was Charles de Montalembert as he appeared at Stanmore more than half a century since, looking up from his corner in his white frock and blue ribbons, the delight and joy and sacred hope of the old philosopher's heart. Probably the ideal life which appeared in visions to the grandfather was very unlike that which the child was to realise. Not much philosophy of that calm kind, no leisure, complete and peaceful like that under the shadow of which his first days were passed, was to come to the son of the French *émigré*, the future peer of France, whose lot had fallen upon evil days. James Forbes, Protestant and natural philosopher, no doubt was far from thinking what an enthusiast for the old faith, what an active and fiery politician, he was thus training. But in one point the old man's dream and hope were realised. The young life was not formed on the model of the old; but the goodness and purity and piety of the ancestor were transferred—suffering as it were a sea-change, into the rich and strange religious devotion of the descendant, without losing anything of their earnestness or practical power; and we may add, what can be said of few, that the innocent child at Stanmore in 1813, the date of his portrait, could scarcely be more true or more spotless than the man who died in Paris in 1870, tried by many conflicts, by good fortune and evil fortune, by persecution and by prosperity. So far as this goes, the adoring love which watched over his cradle was not disappointed.

The book to which we have referred exists still in the extensive and carefully arranged library which Count de Montalembert left behind him, and which probably took its origin in the infant traditions of Stanmore—forty-two great quarto volumes, the long result of all Grandfather Forbes's investigations and wanderings, the record of all he had seen and cared for in his travels. It is difficult to look without emotion at this immense compilation, though there are pages in it which might tempt the stranger to a smile. Love has many ways of revealing itself. For love's sake, the poet tells us, Dante attempted to paint a picture, and Raphael wrote sonnets. This is the love-poem of the old F.R.S. of Stanmore Hill. He left to his darling along with this wonderful work, and many a curiosity beside, the better inheritance of his goodness, high honour, piety, and the noble tradition of a life spent in God's service. To the last his memory was gratefully cherished by his descendant. He was the parent of Montalembert's soul.

The following letter, written when the child was not a year old, forms the first preface to the big book :—

TO CHARLES FORBES MONTALEMBERT.

"The manuscript letters intended for these volumes (Oriental Memoirs, in the form of letters to the writer's family) being now prepared for the press, and one hundred drawings printed for the engravers, I wish to render one set of the book more complete by adding as many copies as possible from my original sketches in the voluminous folios from which the others were taken ; and if my life and faculties are preserved, I propose to add near a thousand more from the subjects which formed the amusement of my juvenile hours in foreign climes and distant shores. This would appear to many a singular undertaking in their sixty-second year ; but I have been accustomed to application ; and when I have a beloved object in view, the employment becomes delightful. Without such an object I never should have begun these additional drawings ; and where, my dear child, could I have found one so endeared to me by every tender tie as yourself ? The sweetness of your disposition at a very early age presents a happy prospect to your parents ; and I trust by the divine blessing the opening blossom will gradually expand into a beautiful flower, and in due time produce abundant fruit. Impressed with these ideas, on the commencement of this new year, to you, my beloved child, I dedicate these enlarged volumes, leaving their continuance and completion to Him ' in whose hands my time is.' That you, my dear boy, may be brought up in the faith, and favour, and love of that greatest and best of Beings, is the ardent prayer of your affectionate parent,

" JAMES FORBES.

" BRIGHTHELMSTONE, 1st *January* 1811."

A few months later a second prefatory letter, written as people wrote when life was long and time ample, with a care and clearness unknown to this hasty generation, describes the " pleasure which I have enjoyed in proceeding thus far for my beloved grandchild." It is a work " which daily convinces me," he adds, " of an increasing affection for my child of promise." And on Charles's third birthday this tender enthusiasm bursts forth still more warmly. "Ut ameris amabilis esto" is the motto which the fond painter placed below the little portrait which he then made of his darling—adding the following verses, in which simple love reaches in its homeliness a certain prophetic height, and shapes its blessing in the very lines upon which the life of the beloved one was to be drawn:—

> " Accept, sweet child, this pledge of love—
> Accept the heartfelt strain, the fervent prayer—
>
> .   .   .   .   .   .
>
> The prayer that He who guides the steps of youth
> Through all the puzzled and perplexing round
> Of life's meandering path, upon thy head
> May shower down every blessing, every joy
> Which health, which virtue, and which fame can give ;
> That noble fame by arduous contest gained
> O'er passion's sway,—oh may thy little heart
> Beat high with young ambition's honest praise.
> Ne'er may'st thou hear a tender tale of woe
> And feel thy heart at rest ; ne'er may'st thou check
> In thy swoln eye the tear of sympathy,
> The milk of human kindness, nor reject
> The humble voice of honest poverty."

This peaceful life and companionship went on till the child grew into early, and indeed precocious, intelligence, becoming more and more the companion of his grandfather. They were much at Brighton ; and wherever they went, the boy was the grand object of the old man's life. After the Restoration, Count de Montalembert, Charles's father, who had been specially recommended to the notice of Louis XVIII. by having been intrusted with the good news of Napoleon's overthrow and consignment to the island of Elba, was named a peer of France, and changed his profession of arms for that of diplomacy. And in 1816, on the eve of his departure for Würtemberg, after being appointed Minister Plenipotentiary of France at Stuttgart, Mr Forbes and Charles paid him a visit in France, where they seem to have remained for some time. Louis XVIII. had been a neighbour of the old philosopher in England, and received him most graciously and kindly, with the royal favour which even philosophers prize, on his appearance in Paris. The grandfather signalised this visit by making a series of copies from his letters, so as to form a kind of journal for the amusement and instruction of Charles, just six years old. At Calais he begins these notes by an account of the famous episode of Queen Phillippa, told in detail in a letter to the child himself; and he describes to one of his numerous correspondents in England his plan of thus transcribing all that is most interesting, " to be preserved along with the sketches and drawings I am doing for him— all of which," adds the fond commentator, " he eagerly enters into, with observations and criticisms not very common for a child of little more

than six years of age." Thus his education
went on unconsciously. And though Mr Forbes
was very candid in his opinions about the French
character, about the superfluous pomp of ritual
in the Paris churches, and various other delicate
subjects, his remarks have all been carefully
preserved. During his stay in Paris it would
appear that the little Charles had gone for the
first time to school; but of this there is no distinct record. It was on their return to England,
when the work of education had been fairly commenced, that the following letter was written,
affording a charming glimpse of the child's
rapidly developing character. The reader will
perceive without much difficulty how much of
this sweet childish perfection is due to the atmosphere by which he is surrounded; but it is
easy to imagine, at the same time, how delightful
to the old man must have been that exquisite
instinct of the child which confers upon so
many sympathetic little souls under ten the
power to say and do things which they never
come up to in their later years. Even the finest
influences, however, do not produce, but only
develop a fine nature; and there is a delightful
mixture in this little incident of the boy and
his training, the real character as well as its
beautiful covering. The letter is headed " Para-

graph of a letter to Eliza," and dated Albemarle Street, 28th April 1818 :—

"I told you, my dear Eliza, that I should take Charles to his school as soon as possible after his birthday, and so I did; for as he well knew at Paris that I loved him too much to keep him from his studies at the Scotch College there when only seven years old, it operates more powerfully now he is eight. However, be that as it may, the day of our separation arrived last week, to me a trial of no common kind, for except at short intervals, I have never lived alone for fifty-one years until now, and I felt it deeply. I told him I would take him after breakfast, or, if he liked it better, he might dine with me and we would go to the school in the evening. He hesitated a little and then said, 'As I am to go, I had rather go at once.'

"We accordingly set off, and when about half-way to Fulham, observing him looking about very carefully, I asked what he wanted? He said he was taking notice whether there were any houses near us. I replied this part of the road was more free from houses than any other, adding, but what can that signify? He then clung his little arms round my neck, nestled his little head in my bosom, and gave one sob, saying, in a half-stifled voice, 'Now, my dear grandpapa, as you have taught me always to speak truth and to conceal nothing from you, let me entreat of you to answer as truly the question which I shall now put to you.' I promised him I would; and I now give to you and Montalembert the very words in which this sweet child thus addressed me :—

"'You know, my dear grandpapa, that I have left my papa and mamma, my brother and sister at Stuttgart, to be your child; and now you and I are everything to each other until we see them again. Tell me therefore—but you must tell me truly—if since we left Paris I have been the boy you expected and wished me to be, and if you love me as much as when we were there all together?' It was almost too much for me; but I could with truth assure him that he had been all, and even more than all, I anticipated. Then said he, 'I am the happiest boy in the world, nor shall I drop one tear when you leave me;' nor did he."

This charming anecdote reads like a page out of one of Miss Edgeworth's delightful children's stories, or, even to go farther back, like an unpublished fragment of some more delicate Sandford and Merton. Just so did the little heroes of the old world, sublime in baby-honour, make their confessions and confidences. There is a fashion in character as well as in costume; and good Mr Forbes was of the Sandford and Merton period, and unconsciously makes his darling talk in those pleasantly precise little sentences which belong as much to last century as its lace ruffles and gold lace. The whole scene is delightful; the still suburban road in the April sunshine, no houses in sight whence curious eyes could view that ebullition of feeling—the child with his little heart full, the old man, henceforward doomed to live alone, with a heart more full still, enduring " a trial of no common kind," but looking cheerful for his boy's sake. Nothing can be more gentle, more subdued, more natural; and yet what tender delight and sadness, exquisite sentiment of childhood, and deep unspoken feeling of lonely age, are in the simple story. It was "almost too much" for the old man; and hard must be the heart which would not feel with him.

There is very little known about this school in Fulham, not even who was the teacher, or into whose companionship the little hero fell who made his first step in the world with such courageous virtue. The only record he himself has left of it was, that he was whipped for running about in his nightgown when bed - time came; a pleasant bit of naughtiness which shows that little Charles was not perfect. His first letter, or at least the first which has been preserved, belongs to somewhere about this period. It is written to his father and mother at Stuttgart in the same carefully regulated style in which he is represented as addressing his grandfather. In it he declares with solemnity that he would rather accept "the most ignominious State of Life than be disobedient to his Papa and Mamma." Thus the Sandford and Merton tone, refined by the special characteristics of this little gentleman, full of high feeling and honour from his birth, runs through his early years, with a reflection at once amusing and touching of the grandpapa's manner and diction. The child might have had a gayer beginning in the young gay household of the French Ambassador at Stuttgart; but the charm of this touching companionship, and all the germs of thought and noble sentiment which were sown in him in these quiet years, give to this prefatory chapter of his life an interest totally different from that of the merry nursery. A shade of pensive tenderness hangs over the young existence, a soft childish atmosphere of musings and dreams. Perhaps he thought wistfully sometimes of the little brother and sister whom it would have been pleasant to play with, and all the spectacles and delights of the brighter world ; but no doubt a certain pride in the fact that he was the sole companion of such a learned philosopher as his grandfather mingled with his love for that tenderest guardian. Children brought up in such circumstances, in the sole society of their elders, have generally a delightful sense of this honour and elevation.

It did not, however, last very long. A little more than a year after this heroic entry upon life, the old man and the child made their way across France to visit the Count and Countess de Montalembert. But at Aix-la-Chapelle death stopped one of the travellers. Alone with the servant who accompanied them, little Charles watched through a dreadful night and saw his grandfather die. It was the first anguish of his life, and he never referred to it without a shudder of pain in later days. By a curious and melancholy coincidence, the only other death which affected him to the same degree occurred also in the night, at an inn, and among strangers. The poor little desolate boy, alone with the dead parent who had cherished him so fondly, waiting for the arrival of the other parents who were half strangers to him, is as sad a figure as could well be imagined; and he makes all the greater claim upon our sympathy from the fact that his little life was about to undergo a total change, and that the influences which were to surround him for several ensuing years were such as to seem entirely contradictory of his past, and at variance with all his previous training. The first distinct period of his young life was thus brought summarily to a close. Mr Forbes, however, had carried out what was the fondest wish of his life. He had made of himself a foundation and starting-point for his grandchild. His example of intellectual labour, industry, and order was never forgotten by the boy; and it was no doubt greatly instrumental in preserving him from the frivolities and crowd of idle social occupations which are so apt to suck the heart out of youth. The old man died, leaving all the collections of his life, the forty-two volumes of his big book, the result of all his laborious studies and researches — his very soul, so to speak — to his darling. Half a century has passed since that melancholy night at Aix-la-Chapelle; but the portrait of James Forbes still holds the place of honour in the library which his grandson has made illustrious, and in the house where a younger generation have learned to love and honour his memory.

CHAPTER II.

HIS YOUTH.

THE death of Mr Forbes brought about an instant revolution in the life of Charles de Montalembert. He went back to the charge of his father and mother—no bad fate, it may be supposed, for a child; but young as he was, his habits were already formed, and the new life would scarcely seem to have suited him as did the old one to which he had been trained. The Count, his father, was already involved in the bustle and uncertainty of a diplomatic career, often absent from his country, and when there swallowed up by the claims of society and that perpetual intercourse with the world which his position and profession alike demanded. His wife was young and lively, entering into all the gaieties which were not only permissible and natural, but even necessary in her circumstances; and the children would seem to have been much left to themselves.

For a year or two we lose sight of the grave little English child, brought up in his grandfather's library, and set afloat on a new world at nine years old, with his forty-two volumes, to reconcile himself as best he could with the unaccustomed flutter and brightness of his French life. But very soon we find our boy again, in a succession of neat little books, his earliest diaries, books already divided into the journal proper, and the commonplace-book of extracts and comments. At thirteen he comes before us in his own person, taking up with a charming childish seriousness that story of his life which henceforward he never quite put out of his own hands. The early volumes do not contain very much that is novel. They are occupied chiefly with narratives of the seaside expeditions of the family—the walks and drives and rides which they took together. Everything is put down most conscientiously: how often he bathed in the sea; how many of these baths were shared by Arthur his brother; how often papa walked with his boys to the nearest height, and how charming the view was when they reached it. The soft tranquillity of those narrow childish skies surrounds us with the calmest atmosphere; and there is a little accompanying volume of illustrations, sketches in pencil of Havre and Dieppe, and some of the villages about. But when the family goes back to Paris, other sentiments come in. The thirteen-year-old boy begins to chafe secretly over the loss of his time and the interruption of his education. He whom Grandfather Forbes had trained to such a serious sense of duty was compelled now to see his precious days melting away in visits, in amusements, in walks and drives and pleasure-making, at once uncongenial to his tastes and distracting to his early-developed sense of duty. How was he ever to become a man fit to take his due place in the world, and fulfil the career to which he was born, if he was thus left ignorant and trained to nothing but frivolity? Already his heart burned with these thoughts, young as he was. Almost bitterly, now and then, when he closes the record of some expedition or merrymaking, he adds, " Day lost, like so many others." The child who at this early age felt so deeply the pause in his intellectual training could have been no common child.

At the same time, his political sentiments were already warmly and strongly developed. When he was twelve, he puzzled and frightened the small soul of his brother Arthur, aged ten, by an attempt to make that little hero swear everlasting fidelity to the Charter. "Mais qu'est ce que c'est que la Charte?" cried little Arthur, opening great eyes upon his more enlightened brother, half weeping, half terrified. Charles, for his part, knew all about La Charte. In September 1833, when Louis XVIII. died, he records with a glow and swell of words which show his little heart to have been really moved, that the king died after a long illness, which he endured with a heroic patience worthy the august author of the 'Charte Constitutionelle.' This is his first distinct expression of opinion upon public matters. His religious ideas must have been confirmed and cultivated by the recent reception of a member of his family, born a Protestant, into the Catholic Church. Charles was only twelve when this event took place; and we find, in a memoir lately published of his confessor, the Abbé Busson, that he was employed to copy out the arguments of that divine and others, upon the points in controversy between the Church of Rome and that of England. No doubt the gentle excitement and enthusiasm attendant upon this incident had an effect upon the susceptible and enthusiastic boy, and directed his thoughts to serious subjects. A year later he made his first communion—that most touching of incidents in the child-life of France. It was in the Church of St Thomas Aquinas, in the Rue du Bac—the church in which he heard his last mass, and which was associated with his entire life—that he received those instructions preparatory to the first communion, which in France are given to all the children of the parish together assembled, and which are much more publicly important than any religious instruction conveyed to children among ourselves. There the little crowd met who were to move the world, and influence it during so many succeeding years —forming ties to the place and locality which help to explain, even among those indifferent to religion, the attachment of Frenchmen to their capital: for few Frenchmen, however irreligious, look back upon this period of their lives with anything but reverential and softened feeling; and to Charles de Montalembert it was a delight often repeated, a new link both in love and friendship, to find that those whom he attached to him in after-life had shared those instructions in the same parish, and had the same associations with the homely church which he loved all his life.

He was fourteen before his interrupted education was really resumed. At this time the Abbé Nicolle, head of the College Rollin or

Sainte-Barbe, who probably had been attracted privately by the intelligence of the neglected boy, or touched by his own unusual sense of loss of time, interfered with his parents on his behalf; and he began to study with some regularity under the care of M. Gobert, one of the professors of the College Henri IV.—M. Nicolle examining him from time to time to judge of the progress he made. Of one of these examinations Charles records that M. Nicolle expressed himself satisfied: "which is more than I am myself," adds the boy. This tone of self-dissatisfaction indeed runs through all the childish journal, which, however, conveys no impression of a discontented or unpleasantly precocious boy, but is, on the contrary, full of external matters, cheerfully material and practical, recording sights seen and expeditions made— though a soft little spiritual sigh, a sense that he is not doing what it is most noble to do, and that life is coming while he is not preparing for it, gives a higher sentiment to the whole. Sometimes he is petulant and philosophical, as when he describes the entry of Charles X. to the Tuileries. He had to stand four hours waiting, and vows that of his own will he will never do so on any such ridiculous occasion again; and then he had to go to see the fire-

works in the evening, notwithstanding that a
great deal of work neglected against his will
was waiting for him at home. " But according
to the old principle," he adds, with precocious
sarcasm, " all that sort of thing is secondary."
On another occasion he says, with fine scorn,
that he is supposed to require *distraction*, and
is accordingly dragged into folly and idleness, as
if these could be any enjoyment to him ! And
then the boy pauses to reflect, saying to himself that he is now in the vestibule of the world,
waiting till the door shall open, and that he
must have patience. Nothing can be more
interesting than this self - communion of the
little lonely soul, pursuing with a devotion and
fidelity, of which he himself is only half-con-
scious, the best and highest aims ; yet never
with any unhealthy fever of zeal — always
happily capable of being drawn away to a new
marvel—with bright wondering eyes always
ready to note and observe everything that
comes in his way, be it museum or country
walk, ancient chateau or bustling seaport.
This curious mixture of the practical and ideal,
this power of interesting himself in everything,
yet through all turning ever with a noble visionary impatience to loftier things, remained one
of his most striking peculiarities all his life.

Such a disposition, however, is very strange in a child; and there is something at once amusing and touching in the picture drawn by his own hand of this young figure standing "where the brook and river meet," longing to push on that soft-moving chariot of the Days and Years, and dash into the bright and busy life of which this was but the vestibule. Never anxious courtier waited more impatiently before the door of his place-dispensing master than the little Charles waited outside that gate which admitted, after all, only into another vestibule—the chamber of education, which so many of his age elude with all their might. How he fumes at the importunate and ceaseless gaieties which keep drawing him away from it! Sometimes he is carried off to the theatre, and is amused and forgets himself; but in society in the evenings yawns his weary head off, and frets against the silken bondage. By himself he reads, and keeps a chronicle of his reading, making up as he best can for the want of aid in those private studies, and with a *naïve* and delightful conscientiousness, writing down his opinions of all the authors he reads, new and old, delivering judgment upon Sallust and Tacitus, upon Shakespeare and Racine and Corneille, with a delicious simplicity. The earliest critical record of his reading—dated from '23 to '25, between his thirteenth and fifteenth years—gives also a careful summary of many modern books ; but the boy's verdict upon the greater writers is more amusing in its straightforward decisiveness. He makes even a little catalogue of the plays of Shakespeare, by way of expressing his verdict more clearly. The "Tempest" he finds "sublime in some parts, but in others ridiculous." The "Midsummer Night's Dream" (he was too young, no doubt, to enter into the humour of Bottom) *un peu ennuyeux.* "Twelfth Night" he finds "mediocre," but "King Lear" is "sublime." "Hamlet," "divine ;" and he describes "Othello" as "*too* touching." Strange little simple record, perfectly modest, yet full of a boy's natural confidence in that fresh vision of his, which made everything new by looking upon it with such bran-new, shining, not-to-be-wearied eyes !

In this book, too, there is a little touch which shows his yet wavering nationality, not quite settled between the French, which had as it were swallowed him up, and that dear English, which had begun to grow dim, yet still confused him a little in the use of certain idioms, and breathed a certain faint fragrance into his speech all his life. After giving an analysis of a serious work upon English law, the boy not quite fifteen adds with some solemnity, "Few works have produced so much impression upon me as this. It has convinced me of *what I had long suspected*, that England is the first nation in the world."

It was thus that the gentle days passed on while the boy waited in that vestibule. How much longer they are, those early days, than the busier ones that follow! so much time in them—time for work, and for reading and criticism and worlds of reflection; and then one's fifteenth year is a year so important in one's life! He muses upon this with an impression of solemn responsibility in which there is a certain awe. Probably, he thinks, the work and conduct of this year will decide his success or non-success at college, and by that means affect his whole career. The final and momentous date of his entry at college seems to have been somewhere about the time when he was sixteen. He went to the College Sainte-Barbe, of which the Abbé Nicolle, his friend, was the head. Though in his later days he concurred in the opinion of many of his contemporaries that the influence of such schools was very bad, especially in respect to religion, upon the boys educated in them, yet he himself seems to have been very happy in his college.* He was permitted apparently many privileges, as the son of a peer of France, at once in favour at Court and popular outside, had a good chance to be—and formed some warm friendships there which lasted all his life. The dearest and closest of these—a friendship most touching, steady, and faithful—was that which united him to M. Leon Cornudet, a gentleman whose influence over him in the early part of his life was very great, and whose sympathy, interest, and affection never deserted him. M. Cornudet still has in his possession a document which he guards as one of his chief treasures, a solemn act of self-consecration, by which the two lads bound themselves to God and each other to serve their country to the utmost extent of their power, and to give all their lives and talents to the cause of "God and freedom." This solemn league and covenant was Charles de Montalembert's work and suggestion. He was seventeen when it was executed; and in the fervour of his feelings he desired to sign it with his blood.

---

* The reader will pardon us for using the words school and college indifferently. Among the French there is no such distinction as exists between ourselves between school and university in training youth. Education is completed at the Lycée or college, which is in connection with the University, and controlled by it.

M. Cornudet, however, less enthusiastic than his young companion, suggested to him that blood thus drawn was not like blood shed upon a battle-field for a great cause, with which there might have been good reason to sign such a dedication ; and accordingly the two names are appended in ordinary ink to this remarkable document.*   It is remarkable not only as showing the fervour of the young mind so early-wise and anxious to devote itself to God's service, but the extraordinary unity of the life which till its latest day was moved and controlled by the ruling principle, the master-passion which thus came into its being in earliest youth. God, his country, and freedom—this was the device which he had already taken up.   It is the music to which his whole life was set.

It was when he was seventeen that this bond was made; and in the very beginning of this year we find, among various meditations in his commonplace-book, the following words, dated 22d April 1827 :—

" God and liberty—these are the two principal motive - powers of my existence.   To

---

* We are prevented from printing this engagement by the very natural desire of M. Cornudet to give it himself to the world, along with the collection of youthful letters which he is at present publishing in the ' Contemporain.'

reconcile these two perfections shall be the aim of my life."

The comment upon this profession of faith is scarcely less interesting than itself. It is evident that Montalembert in later life went over all these youthful records with that half-amused, half-melancholy affectionate pleasure with which we all trace the odd doings and sayings of that strange being who was ourself. Upon this he has written in red ink, his favourite way of calling attention to any special page, the simple remark "Déjà!!!" One can fancy with what tender, pleased recollections of the sweet youth which was past, with what a sense of touching unity, with what smiles and moistened eyes, this was done.

The two young friends who sealed their youthful friendship by the solemn covenant which we have described, went together, as soon as they had done it, to the communion-table, where they knelt together, adding the sanctity of a sacrament to the vow they had made. In the heart of the big *lycée*, full of boyish levity and indifference to everything that resembled religion, they sustained and supported each other in the more serious and nobler way of thinking, which was so rare at the period. In these days there was nothing like popular religion in France.

There is not much now, perhaps, the reader will think; but Lacordaire and Montalembert have both lived their lives since then, and the classes immediately under their influence, if no others, have changed in many respects since the days when it was a wonder to hear of a man, and especially of a young man, that he professed Christian sentiments. These two were the leaven of the new generation in Sainte - Barbe; and they clung together with all the enthusiasm for religion and for each other which distinguishes the young convert in the first warmth of his feelings. How warm these Christian feelings were, and how tender was this mixture of youthful piety and social affectionateness, may be perceived from the following extract taken from the same book, and dated in the same year, 1827 :—

" How sweet is prayer! and, above all, prayer for our friends! What a charm there is in this conversation, sanctified by the presence of God, with all we love! For my own part, I know no more effectual consolation, no pleasure more attractive, than to gather round me in my little cell at Sainte-Barbe all who possess my love and respect, to unite myself to those whom distance and different circumstances separate from me, to transport myself thus, all at once, into the midst of a beloved circle, and to recompense their bounty for me by my humble prayer for them at the foot of the throne of the Almighty."

These pious thoughts, however, are not the only ones that fill his mind. In the same *petite cellule de Sainte-Barbe*, the musing youth feels the fire of patriotism kindling in his soul. "Mourir pour la patrie!" he cries on one occasion, probably moved by the sound of the air called by that name, into sudden realisation of the sentiment. "To die for one's country is fine, but to live for one's country is better;" and then he goes on to reflect what a true patriot ought to do. To sacrifice all his personal likings and vanities for his great object; neither to seek the favour of the mob nor to fear its wrath; to serve a prince even who may have treated him ill, if that is for his country's advantage; to be able to bear adversity for her sake,—such are a few of the duties he thinks incumbent on a patriot. Already it is evident the boy was wise enough to see that a Frenchman who would serve France had many discouragements before him, and might have to serve her with the enforced and painful patience of those who only stand and wait. It is not to be supposed that any shadow of his own future was already hovering over him in his *petite cellule*; but already his much-inquiring, much-pondering soul had begun to interrogate the future as well as the past, and to prepare itself for all the situations which his imagination foresaw.

Thus Charles de Montalembert lived and moved and grew, in the curious, profane, semi-monastic life of the great *pension*, governed after a fashion so different from the schools with which we are acquainted. In the full maturity of his life, when he described the free existence of an English public school to his countrymen, he made a contrast which will recur to many a reader's mind between Eton and the "universitarian barrack" in which he himself was trained. "What a difference," he says, "between this place and the houses where we were educated—true prisons walled up between two streets in Paris, everywhere surrounded by roofs and chimneys, with two rows of miserable trees in the midst of a paved or gravelled court, and a wretched walk every week or fortnight among the suburban lanes!" It is difficult, however, to imagine an Eton boy of the present period keeping such a journal; but the times have changed, and perhaps the difference between '27 and '70 is almost as great as that between France and England. His letters to his young friend Cornudet are very unlike those which we can imagine to be sent by an English youth of seventeen to another. Here is a description at once of friendship and of patriotism which shows the ardour, the high sentiment, and eager hopes with which he entered life :—

" Our union " (he writes) " will be sanctified by religion—without that it would be vanity and nothingness. We will show to the world that it is possible to be Christians without being retrograde in mind, and to serve God with the noble humility of freemen. Our political opinions are the same. We are prepared to *live* for freedom and our country, or perhaps more easily to *die* for them. If Providence calls me to a life less tranquil and more brilliant than yours, I will seek with you rest and true happiness. We will redouble our joys and lessen our misfortunes by sharing them. If we are powerful and happy, friendship will increase our wellbeing; if we are poor, hated, and despised, we shall find another world in the heart of a friend. I whom no one understands, who am devoured by an indefinable restlessness, have yet sufficient egotism to burden you with my friendship, and to force you to interest yourself in one whom you scarcely know ; but you know that friendship is *the only movement of the soul in which excess is permissible.* For my part I give myself up to that excess, too happy to think that your wisdom will preserve me from every other."

Such was the immense estimate which this young visionary had formed of the uses of friendship.

And with all its drawbacks, this life at school was a happy life to him, as to most men. He was allowed an unusual degree of freedom; and, his father having by this time left Paris as ambassador to Sweden, was permitted to pass his occasional holidays with the friends of his family, to visit them now and then in the evening, and to keep up his acquaintance with the outside world. Sometimes even he visited the Chamber of Peers, and listened to the debates, no doubt with many thoughts of the time when he too would take his place there. He found their discussions, however, "frightfully commonplace" —"d'une médiocrité effrayante;" and though perhaps not sufficiently enlightened to perceive the new troubles in store for France, and which were slowly ripening towards the Revolution of July, yet it is evident that already he had made the discovery that many difficulties were likely to beset his own path, and that of his companions who felt with him. The clergy, he complained, did not understand the spirit of the times. "What shall I do?" he cried, after some reflections of this kind. "What will become of me—how shall I reconcile my ardent patriotism with my attachment to religion?" Thus the great problem of his life had already dawned upon him. Amid all these reflections, however, we do not hear very much of his studies.* Like

* It may be interesting to the reader to know exactly what these studies were. The routine was as follows: "He rose at four o'clock. At half-past four he studied alternately Greek philosophy in Xenophon, and German history in Pfeffel. From six to half-past seven, after a short interval of reading, which he gave up to a poet, he did his task of mathematics. At half-past seven came breakfast and recreation with his fellow-students. From eight to ten a mathematical class, followed by recreation for half an hour. From half-past ten to a quarter past twelve, study or class of physics. Then dinner. At a quarter to one, a lesson of chemistry twice a-week on Tuesdays and Fridays; on the other days recreation, in company with a friend. From two o'clock to a quarter past four, a class of philosophy. At a quarter past four, tea (*goûter*) and recreation. From five to six, reading of philosophical works. From six to half-past seven, study of the philosophy lesson. At half-past seven recreation, or study continued in his own room. At half-past eight, supper and prayers. At nine o'clock our young collegian, having returned to his own room, read a Greek or Latin poet, and afterwards studied Greek history in Thucydides or Xenophon until ten o'clock. From ten till eleven it was the turn of German history in Pfeffel or Schiller. On Sundays there was a lesson of Greek and the reading of Plato." This account of a life almost incredibly laborious, is taken from an article by M. Foisset in the 'Correspondant' of the 25th May 1872.

many other young men of genius, he does not seem to have been attracted by the routine of classical drill, which is the same for all temperaments and constitutions. He had done his Latin badly, " as always," he complains on one occasion ; his mind and thoughts were busy about other things.

The duties of a patriot and the duty of a Christian, and how to harmonise these two, were the questions that occupied him chiefly ; and it is apparent that the vagueness and indecision of his mind in respect to his own career had already begun to oppress him. A French nobleman has not the clear and patent path of public life before him like an Englishman—his title is a doubtful advantage, his means not sufficient in most cases to make him a power in his country ; and revolution had deprived the Montalemberts even of that local establishment which helps more or less in the decision of a man's fate. Charles had no inclination towards the diplomatic career adopted by his father ; he was not disposed towards soldiering, like the most of his race ; and from the quiet retreat of Sainte-Barbe, and through all its innocent enjoyments, he regards thoughtfully, somewhat anxiously, the world he must so soon enter, and in which he is determined to play a man's part. The straightforward simplicity and openness of the journal betray the boy to us as few boys ever betray themselves. His innocent eyes, with a little curve of premature care over them, are perpetually gazing out of that *petite cellule*, sometimes with the exaggerated sadness of youthful disappointment, always with an eagerness which is wistful and full of uncertainty. Already, though all his natural relationships remained to him, the conviction had entered his mind that his future must be of his own making, and that his peculiar hopes and ambitions were not of a kind to insure the sympathy of the ambassador's gay household. Thus to a certain extent he felt himself alone in the world. Perhaps he exaggerated the feeling, with the well-known tendency of poetic youth to indulge in the delightful melancholy of superiority, and to feel itself *incompris*; for in everything the lad's aims were fancifully high, and pleasant mediocrity had no charm for him. In August 1828 he announces suddenly that he has definitively determined upon writing a great work on the politics and philosophy of Christianity. This grand idea at once elevates and comforts him, all the more that it demands an immediate sacrifice. He must give up the history and politics of his own time! This he announces abruptly, taking away our breath; and then we hear no more about it. Here, too, in the little original journal the elder commentator has left a smile upon the page in the shape of three notes of admiration in red ink. This pleasant link between the boy and the man may make the reader smile too; but there cannot be anything but tenderness and sympathy in such a smile.

An instance, however, that he had by no means given up the politics of his own time, and that his interest in them was thoroughly enlightened and independent, is furnished by his friend Rio, the future historian of Christian Art, then a young scholar and journalist, with a career still more uncertain than that of the Count de Montalembert's son could be. M. Rio's friends, who were of the dominant party, and who had been seeking some opportunity of serving him, found, as they thought, an admirable way of doing this, on the promulgation in 1827 of a new law for the regulation of the press, by which two censors were appointed to keep the always rebellious newspapers of Paris in order. Rio was named to this office, in conjunction with Cuvier,—a conjunction so complimentary that of itself it might have dazzled a young man. He did not hesitate for a moment, however, to refuse the odious office, simultaneously with the distinguished colleague who had been intended to share it. Amid the public plaudits which this disinterested act procured him, he received, M. Rio tells us, "many private congratulations, the most precious of which to me were conveyed in a letter written from the College of Sainte-Barbe, by one of its pupils who was destined to precocious fame." The letter was as follows :—

"Madame de Davidoff has just told me, my dear Rio, of the generosity you have shown in this last business. Allow me as a friend to congratulate you, and as a Frenchman to express my gratitude.

"In place of certain pecuniary advantages which so degrading a situation might have brought you, you have acquired the esteem of the nation, which, unfortunately, is of the opposite party from the Government. I never could have believed that you had accepted it, notwithstanding the formidable authority of the 'Moniteur.' Such an acceptance would have been a real perversion.   CH. DE MONTALEMBERT."

This little letter proves how real and vivid was the interest which the young student of seventeen took in the political movements of his time—at least, in so far as they were connected with the character of his friends and the national freedom.

In the year 1828 he gained, at the general *concours*, the first prize for a *discours* or speech in French—we are not told on what subject. This yearly *concours* is a contest between the best pupils of all the eight colleges in Paris, and is therefore a much more important matter than the examination of one particular school. The prize thus gained would seem to have been his only great academical distinction. The following year he left Sainte-Barbe. His disappointment at having no prize to carry away with him on his departure is expressed with the utmost boyish *naïveté*, though he was now nineteen, not only feeling himself a man, but expressing himself like an enlightened one. He had not worked solely for reward, he says, and yet a crown at the end of the year would have been agreeable. This is said in reference to the chaplet of laurel-leaves which accompanies every prize on the other side of the Channel—a sort of decoration which would fill an English schoolboy with profound amaze and discouragement. Notwithstanding the almost certainty of his non-success, young Montalembert went to hear the names of the successful candidates at the *concours* read out, and was more disappointed than the philosophy of nineteen liked to allow. He felt it "a greater misfortune than he had supposed" it would be, and looked on sadly at the distribution of prizes, wondering within himself if the successful candidates had really worked more studiously than himself, and contrasting his present obscurity with the glory of last year. This shadow increased his melancholy at the moment of leaving Sainte-Barbe, and breaking up all the associations of his youth. For some days he went about with a heavy heart, thinking how happy he had been, and what a transitory thing life was, and feeling the future before him to be very uninviting. Sainte-Barbe had not been Paradise, any more than other mortal refuges are; he had complained much of the general apathy, and had been forced to take refuge in the society of two or three special friends among all the careless lads surrounding him. But when the last night came, and he thought over his past years in the *petite cellule* which he was about to leave, tears of that profound melancholy which we smile at in after-years, but which is so poignant while it lasts, filled his eyes. He went back over all those tranquil days, full of pleasant labour and duty and enthusiastic youthful friendship. His mind had developed in this studious seclusion, and he had acquired a few friends who were to him like brothers. But from all of these good things, the work, the quiet, the dear companions, he had now to tear himself, and go away to a strange country, to become once more a witness of "the profound uselessness of life!" Such were the thoughts that filled his mind in his last night at Sainte-Barbe. Sadly his existence passed before him in this moment of feeling. Is it indeed true that life is nothing but a succession of bonds made and broken, of hearts torn asunder, he asks? And if it has already proved so in this early period, what will it be when youth is over and the real stormy career of existence commenced, and nothing left to stand between the boy and all these realities that loom darkly around him? His eyes fill with tears as he thus bids farewell to his youth. He begins to grow old, he thinks — "Je me fais vieux;" his pleasures diminish, and his illusions are disappearing day by day. Into this fantastic despondency he drops deeper and deeper, musing that, after all, even youth is of little account, and leaping with visionary impatience to the end of all, that Death which makes everything clear. No doubt much of this was the mood of the moment, elevated into the grief of a life, as youth and journal-keeping have a tendency to do; but it is at the same time perfectly real, and shows what warmth of feeling was in the lad's solitary heart.

It was Sweden, as we have said, which was the place of his banishment—where a gay and lively existence awaited him, which it is strange to find so uncongenial at his age. But gaiety and idleness seem to have been the *bétes noires* of his mind, and he foresaw that henceforward he should have no means of escaping from them. The letter which follows, and which was written at Sainte-Barbe, throws some light upon his distaste for society—which, after all, was not for *all* society, but only that which he found frivolous and unprofitable :—

"As I have told you, I have very rarely, I might even say never, found pleasure in the society which has been decorated with the name of *grand monde*. . . . I feel myself always out of place there, a burden upon others, and only too conscious of being a burden to myself. Besides, I have a most just and reasonable motive for not caring for society, which is, that I lose my time in it; and it seems to me rather hard to be obliged to do what is injurious to me without even finding it agreeable.

"It is usual to say that youth is the time which should be specially appropriated to the pleasures of society. I look upon this opinion as a complete paradox. It seems to me, on the contrary, that youth should be given up with ardour to study, or to preparation for a profession. Ah! when one has paid one's tribute to one's country; when it is possible to appear in society crowned with the laurels of the debate or of the battle-field, or at least of universal esteem; when one is sure of commanding respect and admiration everywhere,—then is the time to like society, and to enter it with satisfaction. I can imagine Pitt or Fox coming out of the House of Commons where they had struck their adversaries dumb by their eloquence, and enjoying a dinner-party. I can imagine Grattan amusing himself, after fifty years of glory, playing hide-and-seek with children. But for an obscure and unknown individual, lost in the crowd of other men, or at the best numbered only among the *élégants* who feel themselves obliged to wander every evening into three or four houses where they are half stifled under pretence of enjoying themselves, I see neither pleasure nor honour in it. I see only a culpable loss of time, and mortal weariness."

The description of his journey is given in full detail; everything was new to him, and he took an interest, notwithstanding that never-to-be-cured despondency, in all he saw. First of all came the quaint old towns of Belgium, with their clean streets and busy people, and the tinkling cheerful *carillon*, which notes the passage of the hours; then Holland, stranger still, with masts mingling among the church towers and steeples, and everything clean and flat and monotonous. Throughout the whole length of the way the indefatigable lad scarcely spares us a village; there is something to be seen everywhere—at the very least, a pretty face at a doorway, a piece of costume, an effect of light or shade—something to show that his young eyes noted everything. On his arrival in Sweden he was plunged at once, as he had divined, into all the distractions of society. At this point of his story we have a little glimpse, unintentional on his part, of his personal manners and the impression he made on strangers, which is amusing enough. We all know what a veil of stiff solemnity, made up of youthful shyness and lofty scorn for conventionality, is apt to hang about the young university man among ourselves, who is conscious of high aims and destitute of any lively sense of humour. When the ambassador's studious son, full of serious thoughts, and hating the frivolity round him, appeared, against his will, in that gay circle, the Swedish ladies smiled aside and made gentle gibes at the stilted grandeur of the *jeune homme supérieur*. Some time afterwards, when he had made friends among his new surroundings, one of the cleverest and most charming of these ladies, the Comtesse d'Ugglas, confided to him the fact that she had thought him *pédant et altier*. "Pédant et altier!" Young Montalembert pondered with much vexation over these words. He had the keenest sense of the ludicrous, and a mind most susceptible even to the gentlest ridicule. And he had been very splendid in his young superiority—he had condescended to note his partner at a ball as "an excellent young person;" he had attempted to lead the conversation to higher subjects, even in the midst of quadrilles and nonsense. It is easy to conceive the intense blush of shame which this private bit of information gave him. But the reader does not like him less that he thus exhibits now and then the imperfections of his age.

Notwithstanding, however, this grand youthful

superiority, we find an extremely lively sketch of
the Swedish court in this portion of the journal.
Bernadotte, the one strong stock of soldier-
royalty which took root under the first Napoleon,
stands out in full relief from the youth's descriptions. The successful soldier of fortune, taking up
with double energy all the old tyrannical traditions of the dynasty he had displaced, liberal in
nothing, hard-hearted and hard-headed, yet with
a certain swagger of false humility, is set before
us in a few vigorous touches. "The king is a true
Gascon," says the young observer, and proves
his assertion by the following characteristic
anecdote : "The king told my father that he
considered himself the natural subject of Charles
X., and that, should that monarch ever require
his services, he would leave his throne to his
son, and hasten, a simple soldier, to offer his
sword to his native sovereign." This is very
fine Gascon indeed, and the Montalemberts,
father and son, were both of them very capable
of perceiving the twinkle in the eye of the wily
old Free Lance who thus hoped to impose upon
them. The trooper monarch and his wife, who
had been an innkeeper's daughter before becoming
a queen, were not exactly calculated, perhaps, to
bring the lighter graces of a court to perfection ;
and the young critic gives a comical sketch of a

soiree, the domestic delights of which were suddenly put a stop to by their arrival, after which event it became *royalement ennuyeuse.* To tell the truth, except on the occasions when he meets the charming Madame d'Ugglas or one of her immediate circle, he finds society in general still far from gay. With something between a yawn and a sigh he describes the *soirées assommantes,* the *bals ennuyeux,* to which he is dragged about against his will. He was still in that stage of boyhood when the grave youth does not dance, and looks with mingled envy and scorn upon those who do; and there is an amusing description of a ball at the French Embassy for which the family and its friends make vast preparations— preparations in which he is compelled to join. The ladies take him in hand, and teach him how to bear his part in a special quadrille, which "we are to have the absurdity of dancing before the king and queen," and which at length goes off very well, he confesses, with a mixture of shame and satisfaction. Never was a pleasanter picture of the boy, full of splendid intellectual assumptions yet perfect simplicity, awkward, standing on his dignity, flushing with foolish boyish shame, suffering poignant agonies of self-criticism; then yielding gradually, without knowing it, to the charm of women's society,

finding himself at last understood, with a glow
of delight, and becoming manageable and amen-
able even to the bondage of balls. Through all
these fluctuations he shows himself to us unawares with the most delightful candour. Youth,
with all its foolishnesses and generosities, is
fragrant upon every page.

While thus, however, he allowed himself to
be gently drawn into the pleasant scenes around
him, young Montalembert departed in no single
point from the higher and graver aims of his life.
He made out a scheme of intellectual work for
himself immediately on his arrival in Stockholm.
He studied the institutions of Sweden with a
gravity and interest afterwards manifested in his
long and elaborate article on the subject, which
was published in the following year. During the
course of these latter studies he pauses to reflect
in his journal with indignant wonder upon the
curious servility of the nation which had accepted
a new dynasty with all the errors and prejudices
of the old, and without its glorious traditions
and recollections. Everywhere he thus brings
the past to bear upon the present, keeping up
between history and politics that natural connection which is of such service to both; but
at the same time it is the lessons and not the
prejudices of the past that fill his mind,—and

no ancient patriot could have been more close
and bold in his adherence to the sacred cause
of Liberty — notwithstanding all the personal
disadvantages of her supporters for the moment,
and all the sacred and beautiful associations
that lingered over the past, in which she
scarcely existed—than was this young son of
the emigration, born to royalism as to religion.
The following letter, addressed to M. Rio, will
show how well he could combat political despondency in others, although he was by no
means superior to its assaults in his own
person :—

"Do not, I beseech you, abandon yourself to
that political discouragement which Burke justly
calls the most fatal of all maladies. Do not
despair of the cause which you have adopted,
or give up sound principles because a generation
without faith and without soul seems to dishonour them by its pretended attachment. I
perceive that you are overwhelmed by the absolute want of enthusiasm and political faith,
by the miserable individualism which seems to
strengthen every day. But tell me, my dear
friend, is it by going back upon the past that
you will find a remedy for this melancholy state
of affairs ? Do you hope to serve your country
by associating yourself with men whose aim, and

the intellectual direction of whose political feelings, are quite different from your own ? Ought you not rather to endeavour to put yourself at the head of the existing movement, to master it, to direct it in the good way, to show that religious faith is not a power that holds back (*puissance retardatrice*), that its progress is less timid, and much less uncertain, than that of merely rational independence. . . . In order that Catholicism may triumph, it must have liberty as its ally, as its tributary. I am convinced that a day will come when this great work will be accomplished. We may not see that day, but at least let us not retard it."

Strange words for an observer so young; and containing the whole hope and inspiration of his life.

Montalembert made another friend at Stockholm, whose influence, acting through him, had so much effect upon Rio that he dedicates several pages in his Epilogue to an explanation of how this influence, at second-hand, directed his life, by turning him towards the Catholic philosophers of Germany, and adding, as it were, another side to his existence. On Montalembert the same influence seems to have acted less powerfully, though it affected him likewise with delighted surprise to find a priest as much interested in philosophical science as any secular thinker, and qualified to take up, elevate, and extend the studies which M. Victor Cousin (then his chief intellectual adviser, and who appears to have taken much interest in his beginning life, though afterwards one of his warmest opponents) had urged upon him, but which, being purely rationalistic in their tendency, had not attracted him. "I am reading Kant, whom I find horribly difficult," he wrote to Rio. "M. Cousin recommended me to give myself up entirely to this study; but I shall not follow his advice. I have made a precious discovery here —that of a Catholic priest who is at the same time a philosopher, and who believes that faith may be reached by knowledge. His toleration is as great as his science. He has revealed to me the existence of a numerous school in the universities of the south of Germany, in Vienna, Munich, and Landshut, which has set itself to combine philosophy with religion— a thought which has always governed my own philosophical studies. The chiefs of this school are Zimmer and Baader, the latter a Catholic theologian and disciple of the great Schelling, who is so ill understood in France."

This gentleman, however, the Abbé Studach, though an interesting figure amongst his youthful recollections, and a friend to whom he continued faithful as long as he lived, does not seem to have exercised any great practical sway over Montalembert's thoughts. He was fond of philosophy, but it was not his special subject. Much more important to him was an influence of a totally different kind, which now came into marked prominence in his life. Among the books which had influenced him most, according to the account of M. Rio, were the speeches of Burke and of Grattan. "The last above all," he says, "as the unwearied champion of the greatest of causes, acquired rapidly the grandeur of the hero of a crusade to the eyes of his young admirer, whose enthusiasm, heightened day by day by the fame of O'Connell's patriotic orations, led him a little later to make an excursion, full of attractions for him, into the country of that great man."

His interest in Ireland, thus begun by means of his grandfather's library, was strengthened by many causes, and gradually rose to supreme importance in his mind. His birth and early training had made the concerns of the British Isles almost as important to him as those of his own country; and he took a hot and eager interest in England's faults as well as in her virtues. And the very air had been ringing for some time back with the echoes of that great struggle for Catholic emancipation which ended in victory for the Catholic cause. O'Connell, the first great visible example of Liberal politics joined with a thorough devotion to Catholic principles, had just carried everything before him ; and his advent and work had moved foreign lookers-on still more profoundly than it moved those who were nearer at hand. So singular a figure in the political world attracted the attention of all good Catholics, and more especially of those who were inclined towards Liberal opinions; and our young enthusiast, prepared by the course of reading we have just indicated, regarded, it is evident, the Irish demagogue with much of that warm sympathy and reverential feeling with which he would have regarded a national prophet and hero. Ireland had, indeed, many claims upon the interest and compassion of good Catholics everywhere. She was the one faithful among the little band of isles which the Continent has always looked upon with curious, half-admiring, wholly-wondering eyes, never sure of comprehending what they would be at. And Ireland was not only faithful, but she had suffered for her faith. She was the only Catholic nation, except perhaps Poland, which could be said to be persecuted. The sympathy which she has thus attracted has at all times been a matter of surprise, and even of offence, to the English mind; but it is perfectly natural in itself. Distant spectators could not be expected to know how much harsher even the severest penalties inflicted by exasperated Protestantism in her day of power were in appearance than in reality; and heaven knows their appearance and letter of law were as bad as anything could be. But if Ireland was interesting even in her passive state, while submitting to the many wrongs with which England was charged, she was ten times more interesting when she began to struggle for her rights. The very fact of the struggle gave her an additional claim upon the sympathies of an age when political feelings were so strong, and when the new fashion of indifference had not yet come into use. The Constitutionalist directed all his attention to the struggle, for it was carried on by constitutional means; the Liberal followed it eagerly, for it was liberty which was in question—and O'Connell and his bands were wildly Liberal; and the Catholic watched it with still more eager and devout eyes, praying for the prosperity of so good, so noble, so holy a cause. Thus it was not surprising that young Montalembert, who loved freedom better than anything in the world except the Church, should be moved beyond measure by this great spectacle, this union of profound faith and burning patriotism, the very union he had dreamed of all his life as the height of ideal perfection. This "island of the saints," this "modern Palestine," in all the purity of an exceptionally fervent religiousness, had placed herself in the very van of the army of liberty; and the young man's visionary soul went out towards such an ideal champion of faith and freedom with the warmest enthusiasm.

These enthusiastic emotions, acting upon a mind which was full of intellectual activity and eager for work, suggested the idea of a book which long occupied his fancy, though it was never carried out. He made up his mind to write a history of Ireland, partly founded upon the works of Grattan, and which should include many passages translated from these works; and in order to do this as he ought, he decided that a visit to Ireland was necessary. This notion, which he entitles a *projet adorable*, filled him with delight. Ireland, for the time, seems to have possessed him. He could think and write of nothing else. Plans for his journey, and for the book which was to make that journey memorable, filled his mind to the exclusion of all other interests. When Catholic emancipation was granted, he became, if possible, still more eager for his expedition, and hailed with double delight the great national act which not only, as he says, gave deliverance to his Catholic brethren, but was at the same time a great triumph of justice, and the best guarantee of the happiness and progress of England. He who felt his English blood beat warmly in his veins whenever England distinguished herself for good or evil, and to whom no local enlightenment had yet been given, bestowed his approval as warmly as he had given his sympathy; and all his thoughts and hopes and plans tended towards the execution of the *projet adorable*, the independent expedition, which was to be the beginning of his life.

This pleasant project, however, had to be given up. It was done with a very sore heart, and with feelings verging on despair. The cause of the sacrifice was the failing health of his sister, a young girl of fifteen, whom he had scarcely known until his arrival at Stockholm. Her sudden emergence out of the nursery into the sweet individuality of girlhood, had given him, on his arrival, a genuine thrill of pleasure; and he had then felt for the first time that some compensation was possible to him for the loss of the companions whom he had left behind in

Paris. Throughout the brief story of his life in Sweden there are many delightful references to Elise, made with boyish affection and pride. When she was confirmed, she seemed to her brother " delicious in her white veil ; " and on the occasion of the great ball at the French Embassy, to which we have already referred, one of the pleasantest details which he affords is contained in the brief words, " *Elise a beaucoup brillé.*" But this gentle Elise, so early introduced into society, had already begun to droop in the chilly northern air ; and after some vague anxieties, which no one cared to particularise, there suddenly came an order from the physicians for her instant removal. This sudden sentence changed everything. It would not seem that Charles was himself affected by the anxiety of his parents. At twenty death looks so improbable, so unlikely, that it is evident the reversal of his own plans affected him more deeply than his sister's illness. There was no one but he to escort Elise and her mother in their toilsome journey across Germany, and the necessity was irresistible ; but, it must be admitted, that he did not fulfil this duty with any alacrity. It was ruin to his great scheme, to which he had already begun to attach exaggerated importance. He describes his proposed expedition to Ireland as a project to which all the prospects of his future life attached themselves; and consequently gave it up only with a deep pang. In the first shock he felt as if his happiness, his career, and probably fame itself, were all buried in the abyss which had suddenly opened at his feet, and, with youthful petulance, blamed Providence, which could scarcely have sent him a more poignant disappointment. The ground, which had been beginning to feel solid and firm under him, again yawned and quivered, and he looked forward with disgust and dismay, which he did not attempt to conceal, to the months of idleness which were now again probably before him.

In this spirit, not by any means contented or resigned, young Montalembert set out with his mother and sister to conduct them to France. But soon these rebellious and dissatisfied thoughts were changed for very different reflections. The little party had ended one part of their journey, and traversed Germany, without, it is apparent, any very grave apprehensions—when death overtook them on the way. It was at Besançon, just within French territory, that this fatal event occurred. They had arrived in the evening, and the young invalid was not worse than usual. It was the 29th October, a day not to be forgotten. His sister had asked Charles to sit up with her that night, but he had not been permitted to do so, his mother thinking her maid a more fitting watcher; but in the middle of the night he was called up suddenly, and, rushing to the invalid's room, found her already in a hopeless condition, and beyond all human succour. With heart-rending minuteness he goes over all the melancholy scene —the sudden excitement and night-alarm, the rushing to and fro, the strange doctors suddenly called, the dreary strange inn roused up. Fortunately, however, there were friends at hand. The Cardinal de Rohan, Archbishop of Besançon, hastened to carry the last sacraments to the dying girl, and to give what consolation was possible to her mother and brother. The circumstances were not so sad as those under which, ten years before, he had been separated from his kind grandfather; but there was resemblance enough to call up many a sad recollection; and the loss of this new and tender natural affection, just as it had begun to warm his heart, was a great and painful blow. The reader will easily imagine the compunctions, the visionary remorse which seized the young man, who had given up his schemes so unwillingly to be Elise's escort and companion. With his heart, as he thought, broken, blaming himself for his carelessness of her, and overwhelmed with his first grief, he buried Elise in the strange place which henceforward had the closest claim upon him. Never was a sadder journey than that which the mother and son, weeping and silent, pursued together to Paris; and thus he began the year 1830—a year of many great events, and one which, little as he then anticipated it, introduced him to the excitements and stormy delights, the disappointments and fatigues, of public life.

CHAPTER III.

THE YEAR 1830—EXPEDITION TO IRELAND.

WHILE this young life had been growing into early maturity, France had been gradually approaching another crisis in the fatal cycle of Revolution — that vast and dangerous net in which her feet had become entangled. We are not called upon here to enter into the politics of the period, which the subject of this memoir was as yet too young to enter upon as an independent agent; but it is impossible to exhibit fully the one figure in which our interest centres, without, at least, indicating the background against which it reveals itself, and the contending forces whose conflict it was so soon to swell. For several years the superficial and unconsidering world had believed that the reign of an ordinary calm routine of life had been resumed in France— that the great and awful Revolution, though it had wrought immense damage, and produced some benefits, as storms do, was yet nothing but a monstrous accident in history, a convulsion which, from the very nature of things, and constitution of humanity, could not be repeated. The restoration of the Bourbons, though many people felt it to be an anachronism, like the restoration of the Stuarts, had nevertheless been accomplished, and Louis XVIII. had been fairly faithful to the Constitution. The resemblance, however, between these two families was fated to be carried out almost to the last particular, and history was preparing one of those significant repetitions which occur now and then as if to prove to men how short-sighted and unteachable, how little affected by the examples nearest to them, and unmoved by the bitterest experience of others, they themselves are. The first Bourbon, like the first Stuart, died peacefully on his unsteady throne, warning with his last breath the brother who succeeded him—an old man like himself, to whom a long reign was impossible—to guard the crown for the baby heir, who, most harmless of pretenders, has done little from that time to this to agitate his country or the world.

But Charles X. was not the man to give much heed to such advice. He was one of those narrow, honest, royal men, who, being absolutely certain they are right, are impervious, and inaccessible either to reason, patriotism, or terror. It is not to kings alone that this character belongs ; but there have been so many kings of the type, that we may safely accept them as its best representatives. The new monarch, a good man in his way— religious, honourable, and full of honest conviction — set himself steadfastly to the work of annulling all the good that the Revolution had done, and shaking himself free of the constitutional curb with which his free kingly action had been restrained. Whether he intended to restore society to its ante-Revolution conditions is a question it is impossible to answer, for time was not given him to take more than the first steps in that fatal way. He attacked the liberty of the press with fierce vehemence, and, though defeated by the calm and regular action of the law, carried his assault to the last extremity ; he interfered with the fundamental laws of the representative system, arbitrarily proroguing and then dismissing a Parliament which disagreed with him ; and, finally, he had the boldness to supersede Parliament altogether, and issue direct ordinances of his own, putting deputies and public alike at defiance. This was all the length he was permitted to go. Had the country been tamer, he might have succeeded in imposing upon her the yoke which twenty years later was placed on her neck by a younger and more resolute hand.   But in 1830 there was a great spring of political fervour in men's minds.   The heaving of the late storm had left still a certain excitement and agitation in the atmosphere, a readiness to take alarm and rouse into action which men trained to long peace and the composure of an undisturbed life seldom possess. That generation, however, had no traditions of quietness to keep it still.   It had seen, or its immediate parents had seen, the tremendous phantasmagoria of revolution, the melting of heaven and earth, the passing away of an old world in blood and fire, the coming of a new, also in blood and fire, the drunkenness of triumph and the humiliation of conquest.   Such a tumultuous ebb and flow of emotion had left France irritable and watchful ; and before much harm had been done, before her Charter —that sublime Charter which Charles de Montalembert, aged twelve, had made his little brother swear eternal fidelity to—had been damaged except by an ineffectual attempt to rend it asunder, the country was up, determined to resist all such tyrannical interference.   The struggle had been going on while young Montalembert grew out of boyhood to the first threshold of man's estate. Though he was always deeply interested in all political movements, it does not seem that this one moved him very deeply. He was occupied with his personal affairs, his anxiety about his own career, and his personal grief.

There was, however, a new element also rising in the horizon, which was to excite his interest to the utmost, and to affect his future life. The French clergy had attached itself to the monarchy with that persistence which has of late linked the Church so often to a falling cause. How the Church of Rome should have so far forgotten her cunning, and that splendid and far-sighted wisdom which once secured her the highest position among secular powers, it is difficult to tell; but at least her faithful adherence to the ancient rules of government has procured her many woes, and may gain her a certain commendation for generosity, if for nothing else. In the case of France, however, this clinging of the priesthood to the Crown is sufficiently comprehensible on the simplest grounds of reason; for the Revolution throughout had been inimical to the Church, had persecuted priests, and closed places of worship, and even abolished religion, in its mad and momentary

fever. It is hard to obtain, and indeed unreasonable to expect, from any class, the power of impartially judging and appreciating the good qualities of the antagonist class which has conquered,
persecuted, and cut it to pieces ; and, on the
other hand, it is but too natural that the spiritual descendant of the priest who was silenced,
hunted down, and probably guillotined by the
Revolution, should regard the posterity of the
Revolution—the Liberals, who inherited its standard, and who were believed to inherit all its
principles—with a mixture of horror and terror.
The priesthood accordingly clung to the Crown,
feeling that by its aid alone could any resistance
be made to the common enemy. Nothing is
easier than to say that the instincts of the priesthood are always on the side of oppression—as
nothing, it seems to us, is more difficult than to
believe that an enormous body of men, most of
them friendly and well-meaning, to say the
least, towards their neighbour, should systemati-
cally prefer to see that neighbour oppressed.
It is, however, impossible, we think, to come
to any comprehension of the recent history of
France without taking into account the prodigious Ghost—we can give it no other name
—which since '93 has frightened and disturbed
the repose of all the peaceful and timid, which

has affected even strong minds with superstitious terror, and which, within our own experience, has made the masses take refuge in a protection they hated, as a child might fly into the arms of its worst enemy to be freed from some visionary horror, more appalling than any reality. This Ghost, with its boundless sway upon the imagination, has never yet been exorcised; and we, whom no such spiritual enemy has ever confronted, are very slow to appreciate its power; but those whose fathers or mothers have perished by the guillotine have no difficulty in realising it, and see the apparition before them at many a still moment when the world laughs at their terrors. The panic of which they were the natural heirs, which had come to them from their immediate predecessors, and had left upon them as it were a permanent birth-mark of the Terror, attached the priesthood of France to the re-established throne with a closeness and tenacity which won for them the double hatred of the suspicious and watchful people over whom, on the other hand, a counter-Ghost of Tyranny, paler, yet still alarming, was ever standing. This element of visionary superstitious fear—fear not only of what is seen, but of what is supposed and remembered—has told far more than we can reckon in

all the French conflicts of this century. If these
Ghosts are ever laid, and the national imagination permitted to forget them, it will be a good
day for France, the beginning of a better life.

Superiority to the prejudices of their class,
however, is not to be expected from any number
of men ; and the priesthood, as we have said,
clung to the throne. It had other motives besides that of political fear. It was favoured and
flattered, was able to blossom out in processions
and pageants, and was kept in high hope of having restored to it some at least of the privileges
and possessions of ante-Revolution times. No
doubt there were many individuals in the
Church quite capable of appreciating the evil
character of these times, and the inexpediency
of any return to them ; but persecution had
wrought its usual effect, and had raised up a
line of martyrs to dazzle the eyes of their successors, and throw a fictitious reflection of
beauty and sanctity upon the cause for which
nominally they died, and of which in reality
they were the victims. It is difficult for the
Scotch peasant to realise the narrowness and
imperfection of the faith for which the maiden-
martyr of his village, or the grey-haired patriarch
of his glen, gave up their simple and saintly
lives ; and in the same way it is intensely diffi-

cult for a French ecclesiastic or a French noble,
looking back upon the sublime patience and
heroic bravery with which their predecessors
died, to believe in the vileness and corruption
of the society which produced these martyrs,
or in the wickedness of any effort to restore it.
Those victims who were "justified," to quote
the old Covenanting phrase, in the Place de la
Grève, justified to many who came after them
a cause with which they had nothing to do, and
of which in many cases they were the opponents;
but immediate posterity has not leisure to in-
vestigate such *nuances* of historical truth.

There were, however, certain exceptions to
this almost universal adherence of the Church
to the Crown. Priests, after all, are men, and
often are drawn from the same source, the same
family, and from the midst of the same influences, which form the ordinary mass of citizens
in every country. At this very moment two
remarkable individuals, intensely unlike each
other, different in all their tastes and habits of
mind—one old, but with the fiery heart of a
novice; one young, but already showing the
sobriety of a more candid genius—were living
in the agitated world of Paris, waiting with
keen impatience for the moment when they too,
though priests, might be able to strike their

·blow for freedom, and deny indignantly the common slander which made every priest an instrument of tyranny. These men were Felicité de Lamennais and Henri Lacordaire, two figures destined to hold the most interesting and picturesque place in the history of religion in France, and to exercise an immense and long-extending influence over the fortunes of the subject of this memoir. Seldom has any national priesthood succeeded in alienating itself more completely from popular sympathy than the priesthood of France had done at this moment; and seldom have two reformers, so popular, so national, so eagerly devoted to political freedom, arisen within the ecclesiastical pale. With all the picturesqueness of a paradox, with all the fervour of an apostolic mission, they show themselves to us in the heart of that agitated world—men as different as day and night, but momentarily united in a generous and visionary enterprise. The moment, however, had not yet arrived when their united, yet different, and soon discordant influences should affect the life of Charles de Montalembert. He in the mean time began the year with apparently little thought or knowledge of the political crisis which was impending. He had been absent for many months in Sweden; he had been travelling, and his mind was more bent upon the one foreign country he had made some solid acquaintance with, and the others which he had traversed with the eyes of a most intelligent traveller, than with the storms which already began to blow about the political horizon of France.

The beginning of this year, indeed, seems to have been a very sad one for the young man. He was alone with his mother in Paris, and at no time were his pursuits and hers the same; he was quite uncertain as to his future career, restless, unhappy, and not knowing what to do with himself. Grief for his recent loss wrought heavily upon him — grief increased by those visionary compunctions which afflict all loving souls. Projects of all kinds, and of the most different character, glanced across his brain. Sometimes for a moment he thought of becoming a priest, sometimes of joining as a volunteer (*simple soldat*) the expedition to Algiers, which was then setting out bent upon conquest. But neither of these fugitive notions were serious enough to have any results; and even during this moment of uncertainty he still carried on his intellectual work with a diligence characteristic of his entire life. He began the study of law, that universal course of learning which a Frenchman indicates when he says, " Je faisais mon droit." Young Montalembert, too, prepared to *faire son droit*, without any apparent intention of using the knowledge thus acquired ; and he occupied himself by writing an article on Sweden, during the course of which labour it probably was that he went to his favourite church to pray devoutly that he might have the grace of watching, and might not fall asleep over his work at night, the only time which he could devote to it.   Happy young eyes — happy, though dimmed with many a gentle tear—to which sleep came with such sweet inopportuneness !   In after-days he worked half through the night without needing to resort to any such prayer.

The article on Sweden was shown to M. Guizot when it was completed, with a view to being published in the ' Revue Française,' of which he was editor.   Guizot read it with interest, which pleased the young writer, but, with that horrible and heartless callousness common to critics and editors, advised him to cut it down to half its size!   This is recorded in the journal with all the injured feeling and melancholy sense of the world's inability to appreciate him, which is natural to an author of

twenty.   He laments that he will thus lose half
of his best ideas.   " Encore une illusion perdue!"
he exclaims, with delicious despair; but, sum-
moning all his good sense to his aid, he made the
sacrifice.   After this the reader will sympathise
in the indignation with which, a little later, our
young hero records that Guizot has suppressed
the latter part of his article, which contained
that spirited and candid sketch of Bernadotte,
which we have noted in the previous chapter.
Most likely young Montalembert was perfectly
right, and it was that bit of vivid character-
painting which really gave interest to his article; but the injury done him by his editor,
and the outraged pride and melancholy lost
illusions of the lad are charmingly simple and
naïve, and admit us into the very heart of his
sensitive and eager being.

Strangely enough, there is no mention of
the existing politics of the moment, though
there is perhaps no episode of the Parliamentary life of France which is so worthy or
so interesting; but the beginning of literary
fellowship with men already famous, or who
have since become so, begins to be apparent.
Though he had resisted and resented the com-
pulsion which dragged him from one fashionable
soiree to another, his disposition was eminently

social ; but the society he loved was one in which intellectual interests should be predominant, and not that which was to be found in the monotonous splendour of fine houses. In this eventful spring he made many new acquaintances of the class we have indicated. He met Lamartine, and made friends with Sainte-Beuve, who, curiously enough, was then beginning life with something of the same visionary religious enthusiasm which stimulated Charles de Montalembert himself, and whom he describes as strong in the belief that Europe was to be regenerated by the Catholic Church ; and Victor Hugo, then the poet of all sweet and virtuous things, and whose mind was also penetrated by the hope of a universal religious restoration and rebirth of the world. There is a slight sketch in the journal of an evening spent at the house of the latter, in which it is apparent that even the young man's enthusiasm for a favourite poet does not neutralise his natural clear-sightedness — and which shows the great writer to us in all the purity of his youthful fame, but surrounded by that clique of worshipping inferiors who are the worst enemies of poets, and their almost constant attendants. At the same time Montalembert formed his first connection with the

' Correspondant,' a periodical to which he contributed all his life, and which has remained the faithful champion and organ of the Catholic party in France. Indeed, his disappointment and indignation at Guizot's baseness are scarcely over when we find him engaged on an article on Ireland, the object of his constant interest, for this magazine, which we presume was published without retrenchments. Some time after he records of these two articles, with a charming subdued patience and resolve to make the best of it, that one of his friends finds the article on Sweden wearisome, and that on Ireland commonplace. This is disappointing, he adds, with sad reasonableness, but better than if his friend had praised him insincerely. His father, however, who by this time had joined him in Paris, compensates him for the other's cruelty by his delighted surprise on hearing that the latter paper was his production. It says much, however, for the twenty-years-old author, that he received discouraging comments with so much patience, and subdued his wounded *amour propre* so completely as to bear his friend no grudge for his frankness.

On the whole, therefore, this interval of waiting, which he mourns over as so idle and so dreary, was not without its alleviations.

There is a brief sketch in the journal of a soiree passed at one of the many houses which he frequented in the evening, after the delightfully easy and pleasant fashion of French society, where the conversation had turned upon poetry. In this discussion he undertook the defence of the romantic school, and felt a pleasant and modest consciousness that he had borne his part sufficiently well. *"Bon soir, romantique,"* one of the party called to him on leaving, *" ou bon soir, aimable homme; car vous êtes tous les deux."* This simple expression of applause pleases him so much that he writes it down in his journal with a charming mixture of boyish delight and amusement at the thought that he has thus proved himself really competent to hold his place among men, and that other people recognised and acknowledged his manhood and talents. At the very same time, however, the lad, in his innocent superabundance of emotion, turns aside to be very melancholy, bids " adieu à l'enfance" with pensive sadness, and reflects seriously that he is now twenty, with his education finished, and the world before him, though as yet, alas ! he has done nothing. Montalembert never enters into the painful self-analysis which fills so many juvenile journals, especially those of youths whose minds are penetrated by a deep sense of religion.

Fortunately this fatal kind of introspection was not congenial to his healthy and vigorous mind ; but in his fits of despondency he criticises himself a little, fearing that he is sometimes *pédant* and *bavard*—that his " only virtue, modesty," is getting destroyed ; and that his judgment, even of political matters, is not so sound as he had thought. With this self-reproach in his mind, he forms an evanescent resolution of leaving Paris, and settling himself in the country, in order to work without disturbance—a resolution which he communicates to his father, but which we hear no more of; and at the same time he becomes conscious that he must uproot from his mind the fatal dreams of glory which torment him ! Happy boy, with all his youthful sadnesses and perversities ! Never were dreams of glory more pure or more disinterested; and notwithstanding the many disappointments of his life, there are perhaps few men who have followed out more completely the visions of their adolescence, working through manhood " upon the plan that pleased his childish thought."

Shortly after, the plan of his visit to Ireland reappears. Though his heart was in it more than in any other project presented to his fancy, he hesitated, with a generous wish to devote himself to another young friend, one of his college companions, Gustave Lemarcis, whose failing health required him to leave France for a warmer climate. The young Montalembert, touched with that tender remorse, which is so beautiful in youth, to feel himself so full of life and joy while his friend was sinking into the grave, made a hasty resolution to accompany Gustave, and ameliorate for him as much as possible the painful path he had to tread. But as this sacrifice seems to have been quite unnecessary, it was not carried out. The summer moved on big with fate, and still many projects fluctuated in his mind. M. Victor Cousin, always one of his advisers, recommended to him a work on the great men of England, or, failing that subject, on the theologians of the middle ages—a suggestion in which there seems a first faint shadow of the ' Monks of the West'—but strongly dissuaded him from undertaking the history of Ireland, on which he had set his heart. However, a decision was finally come to, all other plans were set aside for the moment, his preparations were pushed on—and in the end of July, on the very eve of the Revolution, he at last set out on his long-coveted, long-dreamed-of journey. Probably Count de Montalembert, seeing what was coming, was glad to seize the opportunity, and get his enthusiast-son out of the way at such a crisis; and apparently the young man's political instinct was not yet sufficiently keen to make him aware how near the excited elements of discord around him were to their next great ebullition. Peacefully he took his way across France, got over the Channel, and reached England. There were no railways in those days, and the journey was slower than now. He had scarcely got to London when he heard of the Revolution, and its success. The effect of this news upon him was immense. His first thought was that the unexpected convulsion was a " sublime victory;" and a sudden hot sense of vexation and mortification not to have had a share in the glorious fight, was his first sentiment. For a moment he grumbled at Providence, as we are all so apt to do. Is he never to be permitted to take part in a great event, or throw himself conclusively into life? he cries; and with a mingling of anxiety for his family, who are in the midst of the tumult, and of strong desire to be himself in that exciting centre, he hurries back again to France without losing a day. But his reception in Paris was the most discouraging which young enthusiast ever received. His father, who no doubt had been congratulating himself on Charles's absence, received him with anything but pleasure, and sent him hurriedly back again, somewhat discomfited and discouraged, and full of many conflicting thoughts.

These thoughts were characteristic enough. The young man, it is evident, had already learned to some extent to know himself, that most difficult of all knowledge. After his first movement of exultation and excitement on hearing the news of the Revolution, and almost in the same breath with his exclamation, that it was very hard he could not be there to fight for the people, he had paused to say to himself that the people victorious would not long continue his idol—and *that a cause when triumphant had no attraction for him;* significant words, full of self-insight, and revealing one great secret of his after-life. For he was born to be in opposition —an opposition with no revolutionary tendencies, lawful and loyal as opposition is in England — an idea which France even now has scarcely mastered, and never, except by moments, put in practice. Charles de Montalembert inherited this faculty, along with various others, in his English blood, and already felt its influence, without probably identifying what it meant, or whence it came. "Je n'aime pas les causes victorieuses." This sentiment gained strength and reality after the breathless visit to France, from which he was sent back so summarily. Even during his brief stay at Paris he had learned that the victory of the people, however noble and splendid, carried disagreeable personal consequences with it. His brother, who was one of the pages of Charles X., had escaped through a window, and, as was supposed, at peril of his life—and his prospects were destroyed by the dethronement of his royal master. His father was on the eve of resigning his post as ambassador; and there were fears that the hereditary peerage would be abolished—an event which, if it took place, would destroy his own highest hopes, and alter his position in a moment. Such personal considerations are very apt to make the best and maturest patriot despondent about the prospects of his country; and Charles de Montalembert was not superior to this natural sentiment. Pondering over the matter as he returned to resume his journey, his thoughts were much different from the enthusiasm with which he heard the first news of the glorious Three Days. With the seriousness of a philosopher he considered in the abstract this exciting event, which in itself it was so difficult to contemplate with philosophy. Already its fatal side had become apparent to him. "Freedom," he tells us with precocious gravity and stateliness, " never gains anything by such violent movements. It lives by slow and successive conquests, perseverance and patience." It is thus with much heaviness of heart, with serious apprehensions at once for his family and his own future career, that he actually sets out at last upon the expedition which once was to him a *projet adorable*, involving his happiness, and, as he hoped, his fame. But our young moralist was too much occupied for the moment with a real weight of thought to remark upon this tempting example of the vanity of human wishes. He took his way towards the island of his thoughts, the Isle of Saints, the second Palestine—for so, as we have already seen, his enthusiasm had distinguished that most difficult and trying portion of the British dominions—without either remark or reflection upon the changed current of his own thoughts.

At that moment O'Connell was the chief figure in Ireland. He had gained Catholic Emancipation in the previous year, and this was a sufficient and a most just claim upon the devotion of his countrymen—a claim, however, with which unfortunately he was not contented. To visit this great man, and gain edification and instruction from sight and hearing of such a leader, was Montalembert's chief object; and though his lively and keen observation, and the warm human sympathy in his heart, sprang up into interest in everything he saw and heard, so soon as he was fairly launched in the new country, yet Derrynane was the shrine towards which the young pilgrim's steps were at once bent. There is a delightful description of his journey across the mountains of Kerry, by, we believe, the same bold and beautiful road of which Mr Froude has lately given us an animated and graphic description.* Young Montalembert travelled in the most picturesque manner. He made the journey on horseback, taking with him a little Irish boy as guide, who led him across the hills, and chattered to him with all that ready wit which characterises the nation. The traveller was delighted with the intelligence of the boy, who astonished him by a perfect knowledge of all the recent events in France, and by the vehemence of his hatred towards England. In this locality the latter sentiment, which elsewhere might have roused some feeling within the breast of the young man, who was himself half English, seems to have appeared to him at

* See "A Fortnight in Kerry," in second series of 'Short Studies on Great Subjects.'

once pleasing and natural ; and when the bright-eyed little fellow, mounted behind him, began to chant the Psalms with which both were so familiar, and to waken the mountain echoes with the Litany of the Virgin, his conquest was complete. The picture is one which will move the reader, whatever his prejudices may be. The great mountains on all sides, with all their varied slopes, folding in these young figures, moving specks of human life in the great desolate yet splendid landscape ; the stars coming out in the soft skies of August, at that hour when the Angelus sounds, and the peace of night drops gently upon the weary day ; the clear sweet childish voice, mellow in its softened brogue, pealing forth its Ave Maria ; and the young stranger with this voice of home in his ears, and his heart full of enthusiasm for the Church, the universal mother, and of reverent devotion towards all the holy and sacred things included in her worship. If the heart of the youth was taken by storm, depressed as it was and full of agitation, who could wonder ? The child's litany was more than an act of worship : it was the voice of universal brotherhood, of a sympathy wide as the earth and high as the heaven.

The journey, however, was much more conge-

nial and pleasant than was the scene upon which
he entered at the end of his pilgrimage, where
Montalembert evidently sustained that shock
which happens so often to the young enthusiast
when his ideal is suddenly replaced by a reality.
On his arrival at Derrynane he found the door be-
sieged by a crowd of countrymen in their frieze
coats, full of talk and argument, waiting for the
return of O'Connell, to whom they were accustomed to bring all their quarrels for arbitration.
This circumstance, however, though the din
somewhat startled him, must have been quite
consistent with the young stranger's ideas; and
he waited with youthful interest and veneration
for the appearance of the Liberator. When the
great man appeared, however, he had but little
time for his youthful visitor, whom he " received
kindly," and—probably with a good-natured notion that this was what he would like best—
ushered him suddenly into the drawing-room, to
his utter consternation and bewilderment. For
the drawing-room was as crowded as the lawn
outside, with a family of sons, daughters, nieces,
and nephews—new figures, such as had not presented themselves to his imagination in connection with O'Connell. This was very different
from what the young French patriot and philosopher had looked for, and he seems to have been

completely thrown out of his reckoning. He had counted apparently on making a call only, and most likely on being received by his hero at a private audience, in which they should have discussed with befitting solemnity the great concerns of freedom and piety. But to be thrust among a merry band of laughing Irish girls and young men, utterly unprepared for such society, and to find that he was expected, as a matter of course, to dine and sleep in the hospitable open house, drove him wild with consternation, all the more that he had brought no change of dress, and was obliged to spend the evening in his travelling costume, a misfortune which must have keenly affected a French vicomte of twenty. Charles de Montalembert is much too perfect a gentleman to utter a word of comment upon the merry overflowing household into which he is introduced thus suddenly ; but the impression of mingled amazement and discomfiture in his mind is very apparent. So is his disappointment with the man whom he had so much admired. The political position held by O'Connell was so important an example for the Catholic party, and at a distance was so imposing, that when he returned to France, into the society of those who still believed warmly in the Liberator, Montalembert warmed back into something of his old enthusiasm. But in the sincerity of his journal, and straightforwardness of his youthful impressions, he measured the man at once, and formed an enlightened judgment of him. He perceived instantly that this figure, which had loomed so large through the mists, was not so imposing near at hand, and recorded the fact with ingenuous regret. Something, indeed, of the stunned sensation of one who has fallen from a lofty ideal height into very commonplace reality, is evident in all he says.

So far as that evening went, however, he saw but little of the great man. The family sat down to dinner twenty-five in number; and probably O'Connell, though full of kindness, had no idea that the serious lad, who was only twenty, and a Frenchman, would really have preferred a patriotic discussion with himself to the society of the pretty and gay young Irishwomen who were so much nearer his own age, and so much more likely to amuse him. After dinner the post came in, and the Liberator withdrew to a side-table in the merry drawing-room, and read his papers and letters while the young people danced and amused themselves. But our poor young traveller in his morning dress had no mind to dance, and stood aside looking at the burly figure over his papers with a rueful sense of mortification and incongruity. Probably the young ladies were equally disappointed, and considered the grave young man, so suddenly thrown among them, as a very unlikely type of a young French vicomte. Thus his pilgrimage ended in disappointment, and failed of its chief purpose and aim.

Somewhat disconsolate, the traveller took his way once more across the hills after this disappointing visit.   On one point of his route, the name of which has escaped our memory, he again saw O'Connell, and heard him speak at a meeting, where various specimens of rude and excited demagogues of a lower order filled the young Frenchman with dismay. The meeting was disagreeable, boisterous, and wanting in all true meaning. The speech of O'Connell himself was scarcely more satisfactory. Montalembert found the language of the Liberator to be "common," and his spirit wanting in elevation, though at times there were indisputable gleams of eloquence. The impression made upon him by the tone of this meeting, its noisy enthusiasm, its applause of everything that was worst and most commonplace in the speeches of its leaders, seems to have been thoroughly painful ; and when he heard that he himself would be expected to address the tumultuous assemblage, the young man stole out and hid himself out of the way with a most natural sentiment. He was disenchanted—which is a state of mind very difficult to bear, often more depressing and painful than a positive misfortune. There were, however, other scenes which exercised a more pleasant and soothing influence upon him. In religious matters Ireland was beyond improvement; and here is a sketch, enlarged from the brief notes of his diary, which he afterwards published in Paris, of a scene which, after all his disappointments, no doubt gave to the fervent heart of the young Catholic a consolation beyond words :—

" I will never forget the first mass which I heard in a country chapel. I rode to the foot of a hill, the lower part of which was clothed with a thick plantation of oak and fir, and alighted from my horse to ascend it. I had taken only a few steps on my way when my attention was attracted by the appearance of a man who knelt at the foot of one of the firs ; several others became visible in succession in the same attitude ; and the higher I ascended the larger became the number of these kneeling peasants. At length, on reaching the top of the hill, I saw a cruciform building, badly built of stone, without cement and covered by thatch.

Around it knelt a crowd of robust and vigorous men, all uncovered, though the rain fell in torrents and the mud quivered beneath them. Profound silence reigned everywhere. It was the Catholic chapel of Blarney, and the priest was saying mass. I reached the door at the moment of the elevation, and all this pious assembly had prostrated themselves with their faces on the earth. I made an effort to penetrate under the roof of the little chapel thus overflowed by worshippers. There were no seats, no decorations, not even a pavement; the floor was of earth, damp and stony, the roof dilapidated, and tallow candles burnt on the altar in place of tapers (*cierges*). I heard the priest announce in Irish, the language of the Catholic people, that on such a day he would go, in order to save his parishioners the trouble of a long journey, to a certain cabin, which should for the moment be turned into the house of God—there to distribute the sacrament, and to receive the humble offerings with which his flock supported him. When the holy sacrifice was ended, the priest mounted his horse and rode away; then each worshipper rose from his knees and went slowly homeward; some of them, wandering harvesters, carrying their reaping-hooks, turned their steps towards the nearest cottage, to ask the hospitality to which they were considered to have a right; others, with their wives riding behind them *en croupe* went off to their distant homes. Many remained for a much longer time in prayer, kneeling in the mud, in that silent enclosure chosen by the poor and faithful people in the times of ancient persecutions."

It may easily be supposed with what enthusiasm the young man, mortified by so many *illusions perdues*, witnessed this scene, in which all his power of enthusiastic sympathy and admiration could satisfy itself, without any cold shadow of contradictory reality to disturb imagination. Probably, had he gone deeper, he would have found even there many circumstances which would have jarred upon the high ideal of his soul. But all assemblies of men possess the same imperfections, and it is impossible not to sympathise with him in the genuine emotion with which he looks on at such a crowd. Here is another sketch, also amplified from the journal, and expressing, though it was not published until a later period, the vividness of his first impressions. He begins by saying with a little regret —the same kind of regret which made him so unhappy because he was not present at the Revolution of July—that he had never had a share in any real crisis, any period of special and solemn excitement, in Ireland :—

"I have only shared her daily piety," he goes on; "I have but seen in passing her habitual trials and virtues. Often on Sunday, when entering an Irish town, I have seen the streets encumbered with kneeling figures of labouring men in all directions turning their looks always towards some low doorway, some obscure lane which led to the Catholic chapel, built behind the houses in those times of persecution when the exercise of that worship was treason. The immense crowd which endeavoured to force an entrance into the narrow and hidden interior prevented the approach of two-thirds of the faithful ; but they knew that mass was being said, and they knelt in all the surrounding streets, joining themselves in spirit to the priest of the Most High. Very often I have mixed with them, and enjoyed their looks of astonishment when they saw a stranger, a man not poor like themselves, taking the holy water with them and bowing before their altar. And often also, from the gallery reserved for the women, I have contemplated one of the most curious sights which it is possible to imagine—the nave of the Catholic chapel during the sermon. This part of the church was given up to men ; there were

no seats, and the population crowded into it
in floods, each tide rising higher, till the first
comers were pushed forward against the altar-
rails, and so crowded together that they could
not move a limb. All that could be seen of
them was a moving mass of dark-haired heads,
so close together that one could have walked
across them without danger. From moment to
moment this mass moved and wavered, long
groans and deep sighs became audible ; some
dried their eyes, some beat their breasts ; every
gesture of the preacher was understood on the
instant, and the impression produced was not
concealed. A cry of love or of grief answered
each of his entreaties, each of his reproaches.
The spectator saw that it was a father speaking
to his children, and that the children loved their
father."

Curiously enough, this is perhaps the subject
of Montalembert's eloquence which the English reader will feel least moved by. Who is
there of us who has not seen similar sights in
Italy, and been similarly touched by them ? But
when we remember how much political use has
been made of these sermons, and how little they
have done for the real dignity and advancement
of Ireland, that chill falls upon us which so often

damps the enthusiasm with which, being sadly behind the scenes, we hear of our next neighbour's noble doings. But Ireland was a distant and a foreign country to the young Frenchman; and in a scene which appealed so completely to his sympathies it would be hard to expect him to descend into the depths and note all that was to be said on the other side. In his 'Lettre sur le Catholicisme en Irlande,' from which we have just quoted, and which was published in 'L'Avenir' in the following year, there is the most terrible picture of the impositions of the Irish Established Church, and the wrongs of the Catholics in respect to that ecclesiastical corporation. Nothing could be worse than the state of things therein described. But perhaps Montalembert himself did not see the full force of his own remark in the same paper when referring to the emancipation of Catholics in Ireland, an event which he had celebrated with the greatest enthusiasm when it took place. When, however, he visited the country, he found that this immense event had, after all, done but little for Ireland; "the truth being," he says, " that all the ridiculous and monstrous penalties legally abrogated by that enactment, *were already abrogated in fact.*" These are very pregnant words, and well worthy the consideration of foreign observers. At the same time, it is sadly and curiously characteristic of Ireland, that all the great reforms for which she has agitated, have been found, immediately after their attainment, to be just what she did not most want, and to have done little for her. However, the English reader must remember—a fact which it is always difficult for the insular mind to understand—that on the Continent generally, and in France in particular, Ireland and Poland were considered before recent legislation as being exactly in the same position; equally maltreated, insulted, and oppressed by an alien and dominant race.

From these scenes of enthusiasm and polemical but generous indignation it is amusing to follow the young traveller immediately after to the house of one of those hated members of the Anglo-Irish aristocracy and hierarchy, who were to him the special and most cruel tyrants of that martyr-people, and with whom, it might have been thought, he would have held no communion. This incident, however, recalls to us in the most delightful way the fact that our hero was but twenty, with the openest heart and liveliest imagination in the world. He went, armed probably with an introduction, to the house of Lord Donoughmore,

which lay in his way; and here he who had
been so disconcerted by his sudden introduction
to the huge O'Connell family, suddenly found
himself in an interior of a totally different description. The " old lord," whom he describes
as an Anglican clergyman, does not count for
much in his recollections; but there were three
nieces! in whose company he spent one of the
pleasantest evenings of his life. The prettiest
sketch of this evening follows. We hear the
sweet Irish girls sing; we hear their soft
mellow talk, their gentle laughter, and are
charmed, as he is, by all their winning ways.
When the music is over, he reads poetry
to them, and they quote to him their favourite passages. Never was there such a delightful night. When he goes to his room, it is
with his head full of these charming sisters.
The worst is that he does not quite know which
one he likes best; but after much musing he at
last comes to a decision. In a few words the
young diarist sets all this delightful youthful
vision, with its soft haze of excitement, its
incipient liking and tender touch of possible
romance before us. Next morning he goes
down-stairs, with a strong hope that the old
lord may ask him to prolong his visit. But,
alas! all the hints he can give are not sufficient

to elicit the hoped-for invitation. The old lord perhaps was afraid of the effect upon his wards of this delightful young Frenchman; for Montalembert records with much vexation, that the presence of his host prevented him even at the moment of leave-taking from telling the young ladies how sorry he was to go away, and how much he hoped to see them again. As our traveller, however, departed with a sigh, he said to himself sadly that perhaps on the whole this unusual want of hospitality was "for the best." For it is so easy to fall in love; and the after-steps are not so easy. As it was, fortunately, he had been struck only by the lightest glancing arrow—there had been no time to inflict a very deep or lasting wound.

From this charming scene, which is a digression, and comes in by the way, young Montalembert went to Maynooth, and to the house of the Duke of Leinster hard by. There, too, there were fair ladies and much fine company; but even with this temptation so close at hand, it was the society of the priests which pleased him most. There were some accomplished and eminent men then in the higher ranks of the priesthood in Ireland, who divined the powers and were moved by the fresh enthusiasm of this young champion of the faith. Two of these, Archbishop Murray of Dublin, and Dr Doyle the Bishop of Kildare, were at Maynooth during his visit there, and the young man was affected to tears when one of these gentlemen proposed that his health should be drunk by the party at the college table. The honour of being thus highly thought of by men whom he held in so much reverence, filled him at once with humility and with a modest pride. This is the last chapter of his Irish expedition, and lovingly he lingers over it—wavering between the ducal house close by, with all its festivities, and the bare rooms of the college, where he could talk freely of those subjects which were to him already the most important in the world—the best way of benefiting and elevating a people, and of spreading everywhere the beneficent influence of the true faith.

He left Ireland in September, having passed there "two of the happiest months of my life." His sorrow in leaving it, however, is increased by the most characteristic regret, one which reveals the young man's tender and friendly nature in the most engaging way. Two things have been wanting to him to make his enjoyment perfect. He has had no friend travelling with him, to whom he could talk afterwards of dear Ireland; and he has left behind him no enduring ties of friendship. Every one whom he met has been very kind, hospitable, and flattering; but the young friendly soul cannot bear to think that he has left the beautiful country and its delightful people without leaving any seed of life-long attachment and fellowship behind. This gives him a visionary sense of desolation as he leaves its pleasant shores. He looks back sadly upon the island, which he has gone through only like some bright bird of passage, to be forgotten the moment he is out of sight. This very fanciful sorrow is a real grief to him. Another matter which he regrets, but with less seriousness, is the fact that he has acquired no materials for his proposed History of Ireland. But, on the other hand, the advantages of the journey have been great. These two months represent ten years of freedom and power, he says, with a high swell of enthusiasm and emotion in his heart.

And there can be very little doubt that this expedition was of the utmost consequence in the formation of his mind and direction of all his future labours. He had already discovered in himself that inclination towards the unfortunate which is one of the highest principles of chivalry, though not always perhaps a perfectly safe guide either in politics or in morals; and it is not difficult to understand the overwhelming impression which must have been made upon such a mind by the aspect of affairs in Ireland. Naturally, as we all do, the young observer approached these affairs not impartially but from one side, and with all the strenuous certainty of his age felt his standpoint to be the only just one. From that standing-ground he saw a heretic Church, without any pretension to be the Church of the people, enjoying large ecclesiastical revenues, assembling its half-dozen worshippers in vast churches meant for the masses, and enjoying all the consideration and importance due to a great hierarchy ; while, on the other side, the true Church in modest frieze —while the other wore purple and fine linen— said its multitudinous prayers in the mud, under thatched roofs, in poverty and wretchedness, with a fervour and simplicity of devotion which went to the very heart of the looker-on. That must be a miserable form of faith indeed which does not, when so presented, attract the respect and reverence of every generous mind ; but the worship of splendid Rome deprived of all ornaments and accessories, and held in miserable hovels amid the barest unlovely poverty and devastation, is always a pathetic sight. A dethroned queen cheerfully fulfilling the meanest offices, and working with her own hands for her children, may not be intrinsically nobler than a simple woman who does the same things by habit and nature ; but how much more does her aspect touch the beholder ! Something of the same interest hangs about the hedge-chapel, where, without an ornament on the altar or a change of vestments, the humble priests celebrate the same service which is celebrated under the splendid dome of St Peter's with all that art can do to minister to its effect. The simpler rite which rejects these aids is expected to do without them ; but when Rome, who does not reject them, does without them, even the most unsympathetic bystander must be touched by that evidence of divine strength still remaining in her. And to the young Catholic enthusiast, the nakedness and poverty of the Church he adored appealed with a much warmer and closer charm. Her faithfulness to the people whose souls she had to guard, her steadfast persistence and perseverance, her spare fare, her mean dwellings, her martyr lowliness of life, recalled to him all the triumphs of her origin, all the persecutions she had surmounted, all the blood that had been shed and the pangs that had been endured, before ever she set foot within a palace or dreamt of the Vatican. The sight sent him back to primitive times — to that age of primal fervour of which he afterwards became the historian—to those early recollections which are common to all Christians.   And that impression which is made upon us all by the sight of simple and sincere devotion—that feeling half of reverence, half of wonder, with which the Protestant stranger looks upon a church full of rapt Italian worshippers in those distant regions where neither politics nor profanity have stepped in to disturb their faith— was tenfold deeper in the mind of the young French Catholic, who had indeed dreamt of such devotion as this, and felt that his life would be well spent could he bring it into the neglected Church of his own country, but who never till now had seen with what all-absorbing fervour men were still capable of worshipping God.

Evidently this was the turning - point in Montalembert's career.   He was taken by storm in the midst of all the vague and contending impulses of his mind; and he was taken on the wing with no opportunity to examine more deeply or make out more distinctly all the tendencies and consequences of this great theocracy.   He saw only that it was a theocracy, an ideal government, which is always entrancing to the young soul.   These poor priests, rude, laborious, and poverty-stricken as were the flocks they swayed, were in reality the rulers of that great people. They gave to it all its consolation, all its elevation, that divine element which makes such a wonderful separation between the lowest human existence and the life of the brute. The priesthood was at once the king and the soul of the Irish people. What a contrast was this to France, which scoffed at religion, which hated priests, which considered the word another name for a tyrant, and associated every ecclesiastic with despotism and reaction! Here, in this island of the saints, the priest was the standard-bearer of freedom. It was he who kept the people steadily up to the mark in their struggle against Government—who cheered them, and guided, and kept the fire of political agitation burning in their breasts—who was the leader of all patriotism and liberty. Young Monta- lembert, like other enthusiasts, did not ask himself perhaps with sufficient patience what these great-sounding words meant. He took it for granted that they bore the highest meaning such words can bear—freedom and patriotism, and profound devotion to the Catholic faith. What was it, after all, but his own formula put into passionate and most real life?

Thus, while the young traveller came to Ireland with his head full of a great many different projects, and his destination as yet undecided—ready to be drawn into any generous and highly - aiming movement — loving above all things the good of his country, and seeking above all things the worthiest career, whatever that might be, in which to serve her —he left it decided and fixed for ever, a Catholic champion, a sworn knight of the faith. All his youthful piety, and the resolutions which he had expressed so early, had worked towards this end. But there can be little doubt that it was Ireland which decided his future. He had come to see the Liberator, from whom he derived not very much ; but, by the way, he had seen a worshipping nation, and his imagination had been inspired by the sight, and all his resolutions had burst into flower.

CHAPTER IV.

L'AVENIR.—"GOD AND LIBERTY."

THE episode which follows is one of the most curious in recent history: it is the very romance of journalism, perhaps the only chivalrous incident which has ever taken place in the history of newspapers. We have already mentioned the names of Felicité de Lamennais and Henri Lacordaire. The elder of these two was a priest of Brittany, the son of a family of bourgeois gentry in that ancient and loyal province —who had begun his life as firmly Royalist as he was devoutly Catholic. He was perhaps the most distinguished man in the French priesthood at this moment—"the most illustrious ecclesiastic of his time," Lacordaire, who had no natural sympathy with him and no love for him, does not hesitate to say. Many years before, he had moved the whole Catholic world by his 'Essai sur l'Indifference,' a work which raised

him to the highest popularity in the Church
and among the faithful.   So great was the
honour in which he was held, that the late Pope,
Leo XII., not only sent for him to Rome and
overwhelmed him with caresses, but did him
the distinguished honour of hanging his portrait among saints and martyrs in his own
private cabinet, as that of the only man living
who was worthy to hold such a place.   He was
a man in whom fancy, imagination, self-will,
and the intense logic peculiar to the Celtic
intellect, were stronger than reason; born with
that desire for sympathy which sometimes
degenerates into a desire for worship; with
great conversational powers and eloquence of
style; a man of intense personal influence more
than solid weight; the sort of soul which moves
through the world surrounded by a little phalanx of adorers.   His contemporary reputation
was unbounded, and his character and position
were both full of interest.   Lamennais's signal
change of sentiment in his later years has armed
as many tongues against him as once were
blatant in his praise.   But the story is a very
sad one; and it is not our intention to throw
any stone at him, or to disturb the silence in
which his then brothers-in-arms have shrouded
the end of his life.

At this period, however, Lamennais was surrounded by nothing but honour and universal respect. The Abbé Gerbet, whom Victor Cousin distinguished as " un ange mystique," was one of the high priests of this prophet, leading under him the band of disciples which surrounded the master, and bringing in whom he could from " the world" as well as from the clergy—new souls to join the adoring circle, or to be converted by the influence of its leader. It was in the former class that he must have reckoned a young advocate from the department of the Côte-d'Or, a thoughtful young man, full of reason and goodness, but also of enthusiastically liberal sentiments, pure in morals and character, but Pagan rather than Christian in his opinions, as were most of the educated young men of the period. This was young Lacordaire, lately arrived from Dijon to qualify himself fully for the bar, all unacquainted with his future destiny, and bringing with him all the undeveloped eloquence which afterwards made him so famous. He was without any personal faith of his own, except that belief in " Liberty" which was the one creed of Frenchmen at the time ; but his mother was good, pious, and a Legitimist, and probably by her suggestion, the friend and patron, to whom he had been chiefly recommended, had introduced him to a society called " des Bonnes Etudes," hoping that the company of the select number of pious young Royalists who formed it might do him good. But the Society for Good Studies had not done much for him : and he would seem to have regarded Lamennais also with curiosity and attention, studying with eyes cold and clear the strange spectacle of a man of genius possessed and dominated by religious faith. Lacordaire was not, however, a bigot in his scepticism, or contemptuous of the faith which he did not understand, but simply observant and unsympathetic. "The sight of Lamennais and his conversation produced no impression upon me but one of curiosity," he himself tells us. Up to a certain point his aspect was that of a spectator, curious and studying all things, but quite undecided in respect to religion—inclining, indeed, rather against than for everything that looked like orthodox faith.

It is not necessary for us to describe the means by which Lamennais was brought from royalism and absolutism to a strong conviction of the necessity of liberal institutions for the country, and to share that enthusiasm for " Liberty " which then possessed France like a kind of inspiration : nor can we, on the other hand, enter into the curiously silent and sudden way in which Lacordaire's conversion to the profoundest religious belief took place. This latter event, however, had no sooner happened, than, with the decision and promptitude peculiar to his character, the young advocate resigned his worldly avocation and began his studies for the priesthood. During the course of these studies he had many rebuffs to bear, for the ecclesiastical world into which he had entered was as curiously observant of him and as unsympathetic, as he himself had been a little while before of the enthusiastic religion and royalism of the young men of the society " des Bonnes Etudes;" and his progress into the priesthood was something of a struggle—many obstacles being introduced by his suspicious teachers between the student they did not understand and his aim.

Such were the two men, perfect types of French character both, who were about to come into the life of the young Charles de Montalembert—the one like a comet, disturbing the atmosphere, bringing brilliant illumination, disorder, pain, and final darkness in its train ; the other as a steadfast friendly star, full of wise guidance and good influence. He was not even acquainted with either during the spring and summer of 1830, which he spent in Paris. In the mean time, however, they had been drawing unconsciously together—approaching, as it were from opposite poles, one great conclusion. Lamennais's political sentiments had changed gradually and slowly, but in their approaches to liberalism and even democratical opinion had preserved the ecclesiastical colour with which naturally the ideas of a pious priest would be tinged. Probably it was to the work of O'Connell that his full transformation into a champion of liberty was due. Such indirect influences of a great popular movement are seldom sufficiently appreciated at the moment; and these indirect results are often, as we believe they were in this instance, founded upon a somewhat mistaken view of the enterprise which they intended to emulate. In the eyes of the Catholic world — which distance and ignorance of English institutions kept unaware of the fact discovered by young Montalembert on his visit to Ireland, that the great part of the Catholic wrongs, of which O'Connell made political capital, had been abrogated in fact long before they were formally abolished—O'Connell's agitation was chiefly a religious movement—a grand and sublime national effort for the enfranchisement of religion. As such it produced

an immense effect upon the Catholic mind
throughout the Continent. At risk of weary-
ing the reader we repeat this, as it is the only
means by which he can come to any comprehension of the curiously elevated place given to
O'Connell on the other side of the Channel,
where he ranks not only as a patriot of the
most exalted class, but if not as a saint, yet as
a confessor of the faith and one of its noblest
champions. Probably, indeed, one of the greatest of his achievements was the impulse given
by a mistaken conception of his work to the
Catholics of France and of Belgium, who regarded it only from a religious point of view.

There seems little doubt that it was this vision
of a Liberator who should, in the general impulse
towards freedom, win for the Church too a
crowning liberty, that roused the imagination
of Lamennais. Freedom was at that time, as
we have said, the passion of all Frenchmen who
were not absolutely devoted Legitimists. The
Charter—the free institutions it guaranteed, the
self-government which it held out to the hopes
of the nation—was the popular idol. But in the
midst of this impetuous rush towards political
freedom the Church remained in bondage. Even
the men who were content to risk their lives for
the integrity of their Parliament and for their

right to elect it, saw no harm—nay, the reverse—considered it right and necessary that all ecclesiastical dignitaries should be appointed by Government, and denied to the clergy the right to elect *their* representatives, the bishops. This, which every modern government has insisted upon as indispensable to its safety, was a direct contradiction of all the theoretical rights guaranteed by the doctrines of liberty and equality. Nor were these the only wrongs of the Church in France. Prejudice and impiety had imposed upon her a much heavier yoke than the English heretics had imposed upon the Catholic Church in England. At the very time of which we speak it was dangerous for a priest to go about the streets *en soutane*, in the costume of his class; and when the cholera appeared in Paris, the services of priests, volunteered on all hands, were refused at the hospitals, and they had to be smuggled in privately in the dress of laymen to administer the last sacraments to such expiring sufferers as desired their services. Everything was free, except religion; nor does it seem to have occurred to the generality of men that the Church had any right to ask the freedom which every other institution had secured. The difference between the opinion of secular society on this point, and that which began slowly to develop in the breasts of certain religious men, cannot be better expressed than in the words of Lacordaire, who had entertained the former sentiments in the beginning of his career, and who had now become one of the leaders of the movement for religious freedom.

"In my youth," he says, "the liberal question presented itself to me only as affecting the country and humanity. I desired, like most of my contemporaries, the final triumph of the principles of 1789 by the establishment and execution of the Charter of 1814. In this everything was included for us. The Church in our thoughts was nothing but an obstacle: it never entered into our minds to suppose that she too required to invoke freedom, and to claim her share in the patrimony of these new rights. When I became a Christian, this second point of view became visible to me: my liberalism thus embraced France and the Church together, and I suffered so much the more in the civil struggle that I had henceforward two causes to sustain in one—two causes which seemed irreconcilable enemies, which no voice ought to attempt to bring together."

Thus from totally different points of view these two minds drew near each other. Lamennais, impatient of the subjection of the Church

to a continual course of worldly expediences, and
of the fatal identification of her cause with that
of the fallen monarchy, took up with enthusiasm the new reign of constitutional freedom,
chiefly because of the great opening it afforded
for that claim of freedom for religion which he
was burning to make. Lacordaire, on the other
hand, a young man trained in all the traditions
of political liberty, and accustomed to assert
for himself a right to perfect individual freedom, suddenly found, with indignation and
anguish, that the class to which he had joined
himself was the only one denied that freedom
which he felt to be no less his right now than
it had been in his secular days; and with all
the strength of his nature, resisting the idea
that he was no longer a man like others, laid
bold claim, as a priest, to the same rights
which other men possessed. Thus the two,
approaching the subject from different aspects,
agreed in their claim of rights. So far as Lacordaire was concerned, a strong sense of personal
humiliation, mingled with his indignant resent-
ment at the wrong done to the Church, filled
him with vague and passionate longings for some
way of appealing against so great an injustice,
and winning liberty of action for that community
with which henceforward his lot was cast. When

he learned by means of the Abbé Gerbet that the great Lamennais, the most distinguished ecclesiastic in France, had adopted the popular cause, and was about to claim for the Church her share in the freedom of the country, he was overwhelmed with joyful emotion. "I found in him the defender of the ideas which had always been dear to me, and to which I had not believed it possible that God would send such a help and such a magnificent manifestation," he says. "M. de la Mennais presented himself all at once, and it was justifiable to believe that he was to be the O'Connell of France, and to obtain, after glorious combats, the same emancipation which quite recently had crowned the efforts and the head of the great Liberator. The cause was the same," he adds, "the means alike, the talent equal. However, the difficulties were greater for M. de la Mennais than for O'Connell. O'Connell had a nation behind him, and M. de la Mennais had only a little battalion, slowly brought together by his genius and his virtues."

Lacordaire himself had not been personally attracted by the leader who had thus put himself at the head of the new crusade. Their characters and ways of thinking were essentially different; but in face of the enemy such differences disappear, and he was one of the first to enroll himself in the band of Lamennais's supporters in this great effort. The first determination they came to was to establish a journal, the avowed purpose of which was "to claim for the Church her part in the liberties acquired by the country." When religion was most shamed and set at nought, and everything calling itself ecclesiastical was considered hostile to the people, this little group of eager champions took up the despised symbols of the Church, and held them high over tricolor alike and *fleur-de-lis*, binding themselves to watch over and denounce every encroachment on her freedom, to resist every attack, to assert her rights, and fight for them one by one, at whatever cost. They took up her reproach, and made it their pride, casting aside all compromises, and rejecting passionately the wisdom of the serpent, which had heretofore been supposed her only inspiration, as well as the panic and submissiveness of terror which had kept her in the background. No longer the serpent but the lion was to be their symbol. They threw prudence to the winds when they established their bold scheme of resistance—their bold assertion of liberty. Their work was not veiled under any pretence of humility or pious meekness. It was boldly announced as a work "at once Catholic and national, from which might be expected the enfranchisement of religion, the reconciliation of differing minds, and, in consequence, the renewal of society."

Such was this strange, lofty, and foolish dream. How it could be possible to do all this by means of a newspaper, neither the leader, in the nervous excitability and visionariness of his perpetual youth, nor his seconds, in the enthusiasm natural to their years, seem to have inquired. The effort which they were about to make was to liberate the Church, to reconcile the spirits, to replace religion in the position from which she had started so many ages ago, when she was the companion of democracy and freedom, the guardian of all national causes. So great was the vision that floated before the new journalists. The subscribers never reached a larger number than 1200, so it is evident that material success was not in the thoughts of this rash band; but they were ready to make any sacrifice for the maintenance of the enterprise, and their supporters, if few, were fervid, and full of self-devotion.

The 'Avenir' appeared for the first time on the 15th October 1830, about the time of Charles de Montalembert's return from Ireland. He is said, by some writers, to have "accourut du fond de l'Irlande" in order to join himself to this new enterprise. But at all events, as soon as he returned to Paris, one of his earliest visits seems to have been to Lamennais, who made an instant and deep impression upon him. He records this visit in his journal as the most interesting and important moment of his life. Besides the newspaper, another enterprise, a society for the defence of religious liberty " Agence générale pour la defense de la liberté réligieuse," of which it was the organ, was called into being ; and the first connection between Lamennais and his new disciple seems to have been formed by this society, of which young Montalembert was at once named one of the directors. The rules of the association we give below.*

The society was governed by a council of

---

* 1. To endeavour to obtain redress for every act against the liberty of ecclesiastical ministrations, by actions before the Chambers and before all the tribunals, from the Conseil d'Etat down to the court of the *Juge de paix.* In the more important cases, publication should be made of the judge's decision, pleadings, &c., at the cost of the *Agence Générale,* and distributed throughout France.

2. To sustain every educational establishment, primary, secondary, and superior, against all arbitrary attempts to infringe freedom of instruction, without which there can neither be liberty nor religion.

3. To maintain the right of all Frenchmen to meet for

nine persons, of whom Lamennais was president. Never did young man, introduced into public life under the highest auspices, plunge into his work with more delight than did young Montalembert. The mere fact of having work to do was delightful to his ardent mind; and as if the very finger of Providence indicated the path to him, the new paper and the new society had chosen for their motto that old device of his school-days, the first sentiment that had fixed his wandering thoughts, " God and freedom "— " Dieu et la liberté." Some of his friends, it is evident, opposed his new enthusiasm. M. Victor Cousin, whose influence over his youth has been already referred to, and whose opinions are quoted upon almost every subject of importance mentioned in the journal, protested, we are told, against Lamennais's political principles, which had become republican. To these, however, Montalembert declared he had no intention of abandoning himself. Cousin was throughout strongly opposed to the ' Avenir ' and its directors. A little later he is reported

prayer, for study, or with any other legitimate aim, equally advantageous to religion, to the poor, and to civilisation.

4. The *Agence Générale* is intended to be a connecting link between all the local associations already established in France, or which may be established, with the aim of forming a mutual assurance against all the tyrannies hostile to religious liberty.

to have spoken of them in the contemptuous words so commonly applied in France to people who occupy themselves specially with religious matters, calling them *gens de la Sacristie;* and even in a moment of exasperation went so far as to say that he would have them all shot, had he the power, as disturbers of the public peace. To this petulant expression of wrath, however, it is evident young Montalembert paid no heed; and he seems to have been left in freedom by his parents to act as he thought best. His father, who had by this time formally resigned his embassy, was living in Paris, apparently to some extent withdrawn from public life; and, at all events, the new circle of friends who now surrounded his son were entirely out of the way of the courtly diplomate. They were men without secular distinction of any kind, and, with the exception of Lamennais, who was no doubt the greatest religious writer of his generation in France, the whole party was young, nameless, and as yet without reputation in the world. A father in Count de Montalembert's position might well have objected to the utter absorption of his son in such an unworldly and unhopeful mission; but either his own mind was moved with some generous sympathy for the same cause, or he was wise enough to let the youthful genius choose its own way of developing. To Charles himself this new and great object in life changed the aspect of everything around. He felt within himself a new vivacity and elasticity, which sprang from his new hopes. A year before he had complained of the monotony of life, how *nulle* it was! what a weary round of nothingness, one day following another, shaped after the same pattern of frivolous occupation and tiresome leisure. But now everything had changed. Even subjects once important to him sank into indifference; he became impatient of vain politics, the different *nuances* of royalism and republicanism. All his thoughts, he tells us, flowed in the channel of Catholic liberty.

Thus, with a sudden *élan* of that enthusiasm which has so often made his race victorious, this young descendant of the Crusaders rushed into arms for the same cause—for the Church, which to him was the purest, highest, and most sacred of all agencies, the most divine of human institutions, the great and consecrated Servant of God, and Helper of humanity. When the subject is looked at on its merits, no believer in Christianity can refuse to admit that these words ought to be no rhetorical flourish, but the simple expression of truth and reality. Whatever the failures and imperfections of the Church may be, it ought to be true of her that she is the teacher, the friend, the help and support of humanity, and that everything which conduces to her free and perfect action must be for the advantage of men. This, we say, ought to be, though we do not venture to assert that it is; but Charles de Montalembert was certain, and did assert it with all the force of his being. For the consecration of his life thus made he has been wondered at by many a spectator, sneered at by some, or smiled at, as natures vary; regarded as an enthusiast, a visionary, a man whose life was a mistake, and who spent all his energies in endeavouring to reconcile the irreconcilable. Such words will, at all times and in all circumstances, assail the man who acts up to his ideal, and who endeavours to guide his life on first principles, setting aside the secondary and all that is born of circumstance. And we believe that no reader who will throw himself into Montalembert's position, and regard the things around him from his point of view, will fail to see that his self-dedication was justified to the utmost by all his principles, and was nobly reasonable and wise, according to all his beliefs and thoughts.

Neither was there anything contrary to the

rules of reason or natural justice in the claims he upheld.

His country had just acted on one of those sudden impulses which, not yet debased by much repetition, still seemed to the majority of men a noble outburst of national determination. Not fearing the terrors which had resulted from the first Revolution, equally undeterred and unseduced by its traditions and examples, France had seized the reins of State out of the hands which had begun to hold them arbitrarily, and had proved that at no risk would she allow her dearly-bought constitutional freedom to pass from her. The State was free—at least for the moment—and why should not the Church also be free? To this claim we know no logical negative which can be given. It is easy to answer it by departing from the direct question—by asserting, as some do, that the absolute freedom of a spiritual caste is unsafe for the human race; or, as others say, that the Church of Rome is bound in absolute obedience to a foreign, and distant, and infallible head, who may require of her a course of action contrary to the laws and peace of the country in which she is located. But these arguments do not affect the principle. They are expediencies, infringements upon natural liberty for practical necessity. In point of fact, and in abstract right, a priest has as strong a claim to personal freedom as an advocate or a groom—and the priesthood in general has at least as good a right to judge for itself in matters which concern its occupation and duty as any secular trade has. This was the principle adopted in its fullest extent by the Society for the Defence of Religious Liberty, presided over by Lamennais; and for this principle it was that young Charles de Montalembert, an enthusiast for constitutional freedom, a true patriot and good Catholic, pledged his life and compromised his future, while still in the absolute stage of youthful feeling; but without ever repenting after of this early dedication of his genius and his toil.

It was in the month of November of this year that Montalembert first met Henri Lacordaire, who was just so much older than himself as to mingle some pride on the part of the youth with the most brotherly love, which immediately sprang up between them. Lacordaire was twenty-eight, Montalembert only twenty; and the young Vicomte, with eyes full of the ennobling lights of imagination, saw his new friend surrounded by an *auréole* of genius and budding greatness. His description of their first meeting, which is to be found in the short but eloquent biographical sketch which he made of his friend thirty years after, is full of the vivid colours and swelling strain of enthusiasm. "Born to love and to struggle," says Montalembert, "he already bore the seal of the double royalty of soul and mind. He appeared to me charming and terrible—a type of enthusiasm for everything good, and of virtue armed to defend truth. I saw in him one of the elect, predestined to all that youth most loves and adores—genius and glory." This encounter inspired both young men suddenly with one of those friendships to which youth is prone, and which take a warmer and more caressing form among Frenchmen than among ourselves. The passion of friendship does not less exist in our more reserved and silent race; but among us it is young women rather than young men who embrace each other, and show their mutual love in caressing words. Such tenderness, however, is not confined to women among other nations. The young priest and the young noble "fell in love" with each other, as we say. They found in each other kindred minds, the same warm enthusiasm and admiration for all Christian goodness, the same eager and almost violent love of their country and its liberties. One can well imagine what a wonderful opening it must have made in the austere life of the lonely young priest

when this enthusiast boy, full of admiration and
zeal and warm affectionateness, came bodily
into it, taking possession of him by storm, with
all the eagerness of his temperament, and the
confidence which rank and worldly superiority
give. There seems to have been no pause or
preliminaries necessary to this friendship. "Next
morning," Montalembert adds, " he took me to
hear his mass, which he said in the chapel of a
little convent of the Visitandines in the Latin
quarter; and already we loved each other as
youth loves in the ardour of its pure and generous impulses, and under the fire of the enemy."

In the same month of November the 'Avenir'
was seized for two articles displeasing to the
Government—articles of Lacordaire's. Whether
these were the same for which, in the beginning
of the next year, Lacordaire and Lamennais
were tried, and which contained an assault upon
Louis Philippe on the occasion of his first nomi-
nation of bishops, it is not easy to make out;
probably it was some preliminary petulance.
The interest of the event to us, however, arises
from the extremely characteristic vexation of
Montalembert that he had not actually joined
himself to the staff of the paper before this
incident occurred. When he read the articles
in question, he rushed to Lacordaire to congrat-

ulate him, but for his own part felt depressed and cast down, upbraiding himself and his evil fate which made him always "too late" to share in any martyrdom, eager as he was to fight and suffer. "I dream of persecution and martyrdom as I once dreamt of work and glory," he says. It is not wonderful to find that, after his acquaintance with Lacordaire began, the idea of becoming a priest, which once before had occurred to him, should have returned to his mind. Before he had fully engaged in the new work, and when he saw with envy his friends undergoing the martyrdom which he did not share, he discussed this question over again with himself—Should he become a priest, and thus get himself too into the way of suffering for his faith? But no: the youth adds, with engaging naturalness, "I love movement and *bruit,* and the world is on fire." Thus good sense and his better instincts held him back from the last sacrifice, which was not one suitable or natural to him. The world was on fire! and he longed to be in the midst of the smoke and flames, getting his share of the scorching and pain as well as of the *bruit* and movement which he loved.

It will be evident, from the very enthusiasm and eagerness of the young man thus longing for self-immolation, yet pausing on the brink to contemplate the pleasant world around, that his view of political and social matters was not likely to be a very impartial one. To such a youth, possessed with that fervour of religious partisanship which is perhaps the most absorbing of all emotions, the common talk of his contemporaries, who were occupied with nothing in particular, but contented with the butterfly life which all along had been so painful to himself, could not be other than foolishness. Thus we find that when he visited the gallery of the Chamber of Peers, where his father had begun to take creditable part in the proceedings, the young men whom he met there, sons of peers like himself, disgusted him with their frivolity. He to whom life was such a serious matter, who had wrenched himself with so much trouble out of the stream of fashionable idleness and gaiety, looked upon them with that doubly grave disapprobation which is natural to a young reformer. But yet, notwithstanding his gravity, he was fond of society always, and not averse to amusement ; and it is pleasant to find our young champion of the Church betrayed into warm though momentary commendation of Taglioni, whose modest and poetic grace of movement was so different from the bacchanalian feats of the more recent ballet. He declares with fervour that nobody has danced like her since the epoch of Christianity; and that she is divine! Montalembert was no Puritan at any period, and the fervour of his religious feelings did not divorce him from the ordinary world and its duties. He had joined the National Guard some time before, and there are several lively descriptions in his journal, of nights and days under arms, when the sound of the *générale* called him from his literary occupations, and he hastened to assume uniform and musket, mounting guard now at the Hôtel de Ville, now at the National Assembly, now at the Luxembourg, waiting for the attack of " the students," or other disaffected bands; who, however, never appeared.

In his thoughts upon political matters he took a gloomy view of the situation altogether. Neither the new king nor the victorious people pleased him. The despotism of the latter especially, in their flush of victory, he found abominable. No doubt, even so early as this, that aimless and unreasonable discontent, which is the seed of revolution, had already resumed its place in men's minds after the first flush of triumph was over. It could scarcely have been otherwise.

When a country has, at a great cost of blood
and trouble, upset one system and established another in a vain and impossible hope
of perfection, what wonder that it should feel
disappointed next morning when it awakes
and sees the world much the same as ever,
the daylight as sober, evils and troubles still
existing, and the superlative as far off as before? Next morning even the most glorious
event of an individual life has lost that illumination of hope which fulfilment slays. So far
as Montalembert and his family were personally
concerned, the events of the year had been
entirely unfavourable. They had made an end
of diplomatic employment and success for the
father, and had shut out from the son many of
those hopes of external fame and progress which
he had indulged during his youth; which he
had indulged—but which certainly never could
have been fulfilled; since a soul so distinctly
born in opposition could no more have found a
place in the arbitrary counsels of the legitimate
Bourbons than it could in the court of Napoleon.

There are some brief but amusing notes of the
literary persons of the period and their ideas to
be found in the journal at this date, which make
it evident that young Montalembert kept up all

his early relationships with them. We have already quoted Cousin's trenchant expressions of rage against the new Catholic movement and its leaders. Victor Hugo, on the other hand, we find, took a lively interest in it, and sympathised deeply with Lamennais. The poet still thought that it was from the Church of Rome that the regeneration of the world was to proceed, and dreamt of a confederation of nations which should secure for Europe peace, purity, and freedom, under the headship of the Pope. At an after-period he is described as more Christian, more Catholic than ever, but very Buonapartist in politics! Michelet, on the other hand, is represented to us as taking a purely scientific and æsthetical delight in all the revolutions and commotions which had taken place, for the characteristic reason that " they make history." At another literary house which we will not name, the lively young observer remarks discontentedly that he had met only " obscurs doctrinaires et laides femmes "—a most characteristically French way of mingling the least pleasant elements of society.

It was not until the end of the year that Montalembert began to write in the ' Avenir ;' but in the mean time he had published several articles in the ' Correspondant,' one of which contained a very elaborate account of English institutions; while another discussed the existing state of affairs in France. In these articles he gave expression to two of the sentiments which pervaded his whole life—his horror and contempt for the sway of democracy on the one hand, and his trust in aristocratical government on the other. This trust and this horror, the reader will remark, were not accompanied even at his early age by any of the inclinations towards absolute government, or scorn of popular liberties, which usually accompany such sentiments. On the contrary, the young writer hated absolutism with the utmost force of his being, and loved liberty with equal intenseness. It was as a matter of sentiment that he took up and held fast, all his life, this visionary support of his own caste, and admiration for it in the abstract — a support and admiration, however, which made him only more genial and sympathetic to his friends of less distinguished birth. No man ever exhibited a more complete sense of equality, or was more utterly free from the very shadow of assumption on his own part; and no man ever had a greater love and reverence for the aristocratical principle. This was one of the paradoxes in a nature full of paradox. A great

number of his friends were not noble, and these
were as entirely placed at their ease, and admitted to the most endearing and familiar
intercourse with himself and his family, as if
they had been princes born; and his quick
and impetuous nature had as little tolerance for
the follies and impertinences of great personages
as had the wildest democrat; but, on the other
hand, he entertained to his last day a certain
admiration for that vulgar English love of a
lord which is one of our least attractive qualities. To him it was attractive; it breathed,
one can scarcely tell what fragrance of recollection, of the times when feudal lords were dear
to their vassals. This was one of his supersti-
tions about which he was weak. We doubt
much whether it ever occurred to him that his
personal value was increased by the fact that he
was Count de Montalembert; but he liked to
think that nobility was in itself a noble thing,
and that to love it was good for a people.

With this sentiment in his mind, and with
that strong sense of justice which always distinguished him, it is not wonderful to find him
putting himself in the place of the Royalists,
whom the Government of July treated with
harshness, and turning upon that Government
with indignant protestations, as he does in the

article published in the 'Correspondant' of the 13th December, though he himself was far from being a Legitimist. Here he asks why commands and honours, which are lavished upon the servants of the Empire, should be taken from those ready to serve France under all circumstances, whose historical names alone are against them. "It is even said," he cries indignantly, "that when the sons of ancient families have offered themselves for service in a regiment now stationed at Paris, they have been answered that the august colonel of that corps wished for no noble names in his regiment;" and he goes on with a passion almost lyrical to ask why it is that the new Government divides the nation in two, and stigmatises half of them as "vanquished." "Where have you conquered us?" he says; "upon what battle-field have we measured our forces? Who among you dare say that we defended the Ordinances of July? Because you proclaim yourselves our enemies, it does not follow that you are our conquerors, or that you have any right to throw the name of 'vanquished' in the teeth of men whom you have only deceived. And why should we have been vanquished? Is it because we write *de* before our names, or because we make the sign of the cross when we enter a church? Then your liberty is nothing but a lying and cruel oppression. Is it because we have served France for fifteen years? But you forget, then, that the third part of the officials of that period were the nurslings of Imperial despotism, the same who now ask and obtain your favours, and who, because they carried the tricolor when it was the sign of a withering absolutism, impudently boast of having been the friends of liberty."

Thus the young champion fought for his class, though he agreed in few of its principles—for his class, but still more for justice and the equal distribution of freedom to all.

Nor is his other early production, entitled 'Du Mouvement et de la resistance en Angleterre,' less characteristic. His late visit to the British Islands had not put him in charity with England. But already the fascination which he always felt towards the institutions and social framework of this country had drawn him into such an investigation and comprehension of English affairs as few young Frenchmen possessed. It is true that his own semi-English origin must have helped in this; but he had been out of England since he was eight years old, and does not seem during the interval to have had any special opportunity of studying her laws or manners. This sketch, however, of the English constitution—in which it is his object to prove that the agitation then reigning, and which was finally calmed by the Reform Bill of 1832, would not in any way shake the balance of England or injure her position—is full at once of real knowledge, and of that determined theory which every fact unconsciously shapes itself to fit.   For one thing, it was the opinion of young Montalembert that the Duke of Wellington was the only English statesman capable of ruling the crisis and bringing the country safely through it.   " He alone," he says, " venerated by the army, deeply esteemed by foreign diplomacy, endowed with an essentially military self-possession, indefatigable activity, and an invincible obstinacy and calm—he alone can make head against the crisis which approaches, and which must shake England to its very depths."   He then gives an account of the opposition party, which he does not think highly of—which is distinguished by a total want of homogeneity —but which includes, " in the first place, the populace," the lower class *en masse*, which he characterises as " the vilest and most sanguinary in Europe"—a hard judgment even of our roughs, who have never done more than pick our pockets. The most characteristic point of the essay, however, is his sketch of our hierarchy of national life—the curious succession of aristocracies, one within another, which in his eyes constituted the strength of England. With a visible satisfaction and comfort he explains to his French readers how the "three hundred and fifty families of the peerage" are supported and sustained by "a body much more numerous, and spread over the whole country—the gentry—which is almost entirely master of the soil;" how this, in its turn, is supported by the yeomanry, and by the clergy, who spring from its bosom, and who have entirely given themselves up to its sustenance and support in all circumstances. "The Church has annulled its influence for the good of the aristocracy," he says—and this is the only particular which does not please him; though, as the Church is a heretic Church, there is a certain satisfaction even in its sacrifice of individual power. We do not wish to weary the reader with these early indications of Montalembert's judgment and sentiments, which, however, it may be interesting to compare with his maturer verdict upon English affairs, which was published a quarter of a century later. Nothing could more entirely prove the unity of the man, and the early ripeness of his opinions. There were few things which interested and satisfied him more throughout his life than this theory of the beneficent influence and immense power of aristocracy in England — a theory which perhaps more even than his English blood endeared our country to him, and filled him with a constant interest in all that was said and done within our four seas.

His first article in the ' Avenir' appeared in December. Its subject was Poland, and the revolution, momentarily successful, which had arisen in that unfortunate country in emulation of France. This was soon followed by his " *Lettre sur le Catholicisme en Irlande*," from which we have already quoted. These papers (though the latter is full of statistics and details) are lyrical outbursts of enthusiasm, burning and glowing with the most high - pitched and fervent sympathy for the two typical Catholic nations, which always continued the special objects of his love. Things were going well in Poland at the moment, and it is a cry of joy which the young champion of all the unfortunate shouts forth to earth and heaven. " At last she has uttered her cry of awakening, at last she has shaken off her chains, and threatens with them the head of her barbarous oppressors, this proud and generous Poland, so slandered, so oppressed, so dear to all free and Catholic hearts ! " " Who is he," adds the young man in his ecstasy, " with the heart of a man in his breast, who does not feel it beat with joy at the news of the holy revolt of the Poles? and we Catholics, with what a transport of happiness, and at the same time with what pious seriousness, ought we to receive this new and wonderful answer of God to our long prayers!" There is a breathless rush of words, a flow and fulness of enthusiasm, in everything he says, which carry the reader along at racing speed, till he grows almost as breathless as the young writer, who has no pity for his slower pace. The style, though not yet formed in all the suave and flowing grace of its maturer expression, already contains all the elements of after-excellence. And even the exaggeration, the hot flush of enthusiasm, the breathlessness of the young orator, conciliate and carry with him the sympathy of the reader. It is impossible to resist the frank and generous impetuosity of this torrent of eloquence. He speaks, he does not write; it is as an orator, not as the calm author of a newspaper article, that we consider him. While we read, somehow the scene changes, the young figure rises before us, with eyes glowing and sparkling, with mobile countenance, and long locks floating on the wind of his own eagerness and speed. Whether we agree with

him or not, we are carried away by his earnestness, his intense belief in all he is saying.
And what he is saying is ever generous, magnanimous, full of the very spirit of chivalry.
If he takes the wrong side by chance, it is only
when that is the side of misfortune. If his
judgment is deceived, it is through pity and
charity, and a noble tenderness for all who suffer ;
and no injustice, no oppression, no evil, ever
has from him a moment's support. His weakness is to dislike victorious causes, and abandon
the successful ; but that is a generous weakness,
and one not found too often among humankind.

It was in the beginning of the year 1831 that
the 'Avenir' came first into violent contact with
the authorities. King Louis Philippe had for
the first time exercised his right of nominating
bishops, and called forth by the act two of Lacordaire's violent and eloquent articles, flaming
with indignation at this encroachment of the
new Government upon the rights of the Church.
It is a proof of the note and influence of the
newly-established journal, small as was the
actual number of its supporters, that it received
so soon this crowning mark of success and popularity. Lamennais and Lacordaire were united in
the indictment, and accused of having used sedi-
tious language, and excited the people to hatred

of the Government and disobedience to the laws. Lamennais was defended ably by M. Janvier, an advocate not in the least agreeing with his opinions; but Lacordaire, who was still nominally a member of the French bar, defended himself with all the natural eloquence for which he was afterwards distinguished, and that ready power of debate which his combative attitude was so well calculated to develop. Contrary to all expectation, these two revolutionaries, who were of so strange and novel a type, were acquitted without hesitation; and thus the first victory was won, encouraging the party to renewed zeal and effort. "The decision was not given till midnight," says Montalembert. "A numerous crowd surrounded and applauded the victors of the day. When it had dispersed, we returned together alone, in the darkness, along the quays. When we reached his threshold I hailed in him the orator of the future. He was neither intoxicated nor overwhelmed by his triumph. I saw that for him the little vanities of success were less than nothing, mere dust of the darkness. But I saw him at the same time eager to spread the contagion of courage and self-devotion, and charmed by those evidences of mutual faith and disinterested tenderness which shine in young and Christian hearts with a glory purer and more delightful than all victories."

Perhaps it was during this loving walk along the banks of the Seine, in the stillness of the great city, with faint lights glimmering in the tall houses, and the stars of heaven and lamps of earth reflected together in the silent river, that, while his young companion, in the warmth of his enthusiast-soul, prophesied glory and honour for him, Lacordaire, turning these brilliant auguries aside, spoke words of gentler meaning, which went to the very heart of his susceptible friend. "He who loved more deeply the joys of Christian friendship than those distant echoes of renown, made me understand that the greatest struggles only affect half our being; that they leave untouched our dreams of that which goes above all, the life of the heart; and that the character of our days, from beginning to end, depends upon the presence or absence of a beloved recollection in our hearts. It was he who spoke to me thus," says Montalembert: "and he added immediately, 'Ah! we ought to love nothing but the Infinite, and this is why, when we love, those whom we love become so perfect to us.'" Nothing can be more touching than this brief sketch. The priest still so young, in the languor of mingled satisfaction and exhaustion which followed his great effort, falls back with an affecting sense of repose, at once happy and melancholy, upon the love of the youth by his side, whom he has adopted into his very heart. To our Protestant imaginations the shadow of a recollection that all love but this was cut off from him, intrudes whether we will or not; but probably no such thought was in the mind of Lacordaire. He had been, according to his own description, very solitary during all his life in Paris, deprived of any *souvenir aimé* to make his days pleasant; and what was his coming fame to him in comparison with this fresh and delightful novelty of brotherly love?

The unexpected victory encouraged the Catholic party to new exertions. Up to this moment it had been religious liberty, as involved in the action of the Church alone, which had occupied them. The appointment of bishops by the Government, the tyranny of a prefect who compelled a parish priest to inter an infidel in his church, and other such infringements of the absolute law of liberty in the persons of ecclesiastics and in the administration of the Church, had been their chief theme; and their claim for perfect freedom of action had carried with it, as a necessary consequence, a desire to separate the Church from the State

by throwing aside all national provision. Now
the young revolutionaries made up their minds
to a further step. At that period, education in
France was a monopoly in the hands and under
the direct control of the University of Paris.
The existence of private schools, or of any
educational institution not licensed and regulated by this body, was absolutely forbidden.
This is a state of affairs so extremely difficult
to realise, that the English imagination, used
to evasion of all harsh and unjust edicts, immediately jumps to the conclusion that it must
have been impossible to maintain it, and that
some manner of eluding such a law must have
been discovered. But the habit of inscribing
laws on the statute-book and evading them ever
after is a strictly British habit, and unknown
to more logical races. Such were the laws
respecting education which existed in France
in the year 1830, amid all the boast and fervour of freedom. A stipulation, it is true, had
been made in the amended Charter, promising
that provision should be made, "with the least
delay possible, for public instruction and the
liberty of teaching." But the monopoly of the
University was still in full force, and no law had
as yet been proposed for its modification. A
study of the results produced by the sway of

secularism in education upon the youth of
France at this period, might be very profitable
and important for ourselves at the present crisis
of our history; but this is not the place to enter
upon it. It had, however, produced a state of
utter irreligiousness in the great colleges and
schools of France, such as few would like to
see paralleled in England. Nothing can ex-
ceed the warmth with which men of any marked
religious feeling speak on this subject—and
the personal conviction with which the elder
generation who passed through it, recall to each
other, as a recollection shared by all, the evil
influences which thus surrounded their youth.
Lacordaire records of himself that he left college
with "religion destroyed" in his soul. He had,
"like almost all the youths of his period, lost
his faith at school." And it is with all the
confidence of a man speaking of facts known
to his hearers, and which no one can gainsay,
that Montalembert, some time later, gives the
following sketch of the habitual influence of the
Lycée, prefacing it with the notable words, *Vous
le savez.* It was a subject on which all were
equally well informed.

"Is there," he says, "a single establishment of
the University where a Christian child can live
in the exercise of faith ? Does not a contagious

doubt, a cold and tenacious impiety, reign over all these young souls whom she pretends to instruct? Are they not too often either polluted, or petrified, or frozen? Is not the most flagrant, the most monstrous, the most unnatural immorality inscribed in the records of every college, and in the recollections of every child who has passed as much as eight days there?"

It may be said that accusations as trenchant have been made against our own public schools and all great institutions where boys are massed together. But at least an alarmed English parent has always had an alternative in his power. The French father, however, had no alternative. The Lycée was his sole resource. If he conscientiously desired religious instruction for his son, his only chance was to put that son in the garb of a seminarist, and send him, under this false pretence, to a purely ecclesiastical academy—an expedient against which an honest man naturally revolted, and which few high-spirited boys were likely to bear. This was the wrong against which the young champions of religious liberty now commenced their crusade. The form which their assault took was one directly prompted and suggested by that work of O'Connell which influenced them so greatly. They took a step which, though perfectly legitimate in itself, was wrong in the eye of the law; not with the hope of successfully resisting that law, but in order to point out the hardship and wrong of it by the proceedings which would inevitably be taken against them. This kind of opposition was totally new in France, and took the world altogether by surprise. It does not appear that Lamennais, whom they called their master, had anything to do with this digression in their broader career. The originators of the enterprise and its executants were Lacordaire and Montalembert alone.

Their immediate stimulus to action was the interference of the authorities of the University with certain small schools in Lyons, where the choristers received from the priests a gratuitous education. These schools were summarily closed by the Rector of the Academy of Lyons, acting under orders from his chief; and the wrong was so patent and unmistakable that the promotors of the new agitation seized upon it as the foundation of their resistance.

In order to try this issue, the young men opened a little school in the beginning of May 1831 in Paris. Before taking this step, the staff of the 'Avenir,' headed by Lamennais, had addressed a petition to the Chamber of Peers, which was presented by the Count de Montalembert, praying that the promise of the Charter should be carried out. This petition produced no response either from the Minister or the Chamber; and having thus found the uselessness of words, the young reformers proceeded to demonstrate to all France the oppressive character of the restriction under which they lay, and their own regard for freedom in this particular. Their school was opened on the 7th of May, in a room in the Rue des Arts. There is something which, without feeling anything but respect for the chief actors in the scene, we may almost call comic in this curious incident —serio-comic, with a certain grandiloquence in it, and that absence of all sense of the humorous in the situation, which makes our neighbours on the other side of the Channel go seriously through many episodes, the effect of which would, in our hands, be spoilt by ill-timed laughter. Lacordaire and his friends—for there was a third gentleman, M. de Coux, associated with the two principals—had, we may presume, no hope whatever of being permitted to continue their school, any more, as they would themselves have explained, than O'Connell had of securing a seat in Parliament by his first election; therefore the little scene which follows

was not much more than a piece of grave acting. The school was opened solemnly by an
address from Lacordaire, which was applauded
to the echo by a company of his supporters,
chiefly young men, who had offered, had there
been any call for their services, an hour of their
time daily to help on the new institution.
After this enthusiastic opening the school began
next morning, and twelve children presented
themselves—not enough to prove that the services of the volunteer teachers were very necessary, but enough to establish their principle,
which was all that was wanted. The morning
passed over quietly; and no doubt the little
pupils must have opened great eyes of astonishment at the singular devotion shown towards
them by these three very exceptional schoolmasters. In the afternoon, however, the proceedings were interrupted by the entrance of a
commissary of police, followed by three policemen, who intimated their intention of closing
the school. Lacordaire, who had everything
prepared for such an emergency, immediately
produced a protest, which he and his colleagues
signed. Then, without taking further notice of
their visitors, they proceeded to set the lessons
for next day, while the astonished policemen
looked on. We quote the account of the scene

which followed from the volume entitled 'M. de Montalembert, et extraits de ses Œuvres,' lately published in a series entitled the 'Gloires du Catholicisme au XIXme. Siècle,' by the Abbé Dourlens.

"Surprised by this resistance, the commissary of police cried loudly, 'In the name of the law I declare the school closed; and I warn the children not to return until the decision of justice has been pronounced.'

"'The hour of dismissal having come,' said Lacordaire, gravely addressing his pupils, 'we will now pray together, and separate.'

"All then knelt, and repeated a prayer to the Holy Virgin. The commissary and his agents, standing still, regarded this scene with the deepest amazement.

"The next day the children returned, and so did the commissary. As on the preceding evening, he summoned the teachers to withdraw, but when they referred him to their protest he turned to the children.

"'In the name of the law,' he said, with energy, 'I command you to retire.'

"'And I,' said Lacordaire, 'in the name of your parents, whose authority I have, I require you to remain.'

"'Once more, in the name of the law,' cried the commissary, with impatience, 'I summon you to go away.'

"'And I,' repeated Lacordaire, with calm firmness, 'in the name of the authority which your parents have confided to me, I command you to stay where you are.'

"These words were repeated a third time on both sides. The children, encouraged by the looks and gestures of their masters, remained intrepidly in their places, and cried unanimously, 'We will remain—we will remain!'

"The policemen had finally to employ force to empty the room. Lacordaire resisted, and was the last to be expelled. Whenever he had been drawn out of the room, seals were placed on the door of the school, and the three improvised schoolmasters were placed at the bar of the Police Correctionelle."

Curious scene, in which the twelve little *gamins*, prematurely polemical, no doubt, played their part of resistance with intense enjoyment, and which the young martyrs must also to some extent have enjoyed. It was a struggle for principle, and was meant most seriously by all parties concerned; but yet we wonder whether there was not a certain lurking laughter in our young Vicomte's blue eyes. Enthusiasm, however, and the high strain of religio-political feeling, seldom generate humour, which, besides, is not a foremost quality of youth; but with all tenderness for these sublime young sufferers, we at least may be permitted a smile.

This was to young Montalembert one of those epochs in which, to balance the general uniformity of existence, life is nothing but a string of important events. He had scarcely got himself into the heat of this combat when the death of his father raised him from a secondary position to that of a peer of France, representing a well-known name and holding an important position. The grief was a great one to his sensitive spirit, especially as it was evident that there was a certain *rapprochement* of ideas between the father and son, at least at the end of the Count de Montalembert's life, and that he had taken a fatherly pride and satisfaction in the commencement of life made by his young representative. Now, however, the young man had to step into his father's place, feeling the new vacancy and strangeness, and his increased loneliness, with the warmth which was natural to all his feelings. But in the haste and din of the conflict then raging, there was something which lulled and silenced the outcries of personal pain ; and as this loss occurred before the trial of the young revolutionaries, the first step taken by Montalembert in his new character was to appeal that he might be tried by his peers, according to the law of France—a step which threw a still greater glow of romantic distinction over the story, and called all eyes to the novel appearance at the bar of the Chamber of Peers of the three *accusés*, indicted for having opened a free school for poor children in the midst of Paris. The advantage of thus calling public attention to their cause was perhaps greater in appearance than in reality ; but in any way in which it can be looked at, the scene was a striking one, and well calculated to inspire the imagination ; and the judges were probably the most favourable who could have been found in France, well disposed towards the rebel, who was one of themselves, and touched by the feeling of his recent loss, and by the fact that a public appearance was thus demanded of him before the natural tears had dried in his eyes. According to the law, his two fellow-culprits accompanied him to this higher tribunal; and here the *début* at once of Lacordaire and Montalembert took place in the great world. Their audience included all that was noblest in

France; men prepared—by those centuries of education which cultivate in a race a deepened sense, at least, of all the superficial graces of oratory and diction—to be influenced by the fresh eloquence of the two speakers who were to count thereafter among the greatest orators of their time. Lacordaire spoke first, a bold and fine address, in which he drew a daring parallel between the Government which had taken advantage of a right accorded by the Charter, but not formulated in a law, to impeach the previous ministers, and himself who had used a similar right for a benevolent purpose. "If they could do it, so could I," said the brave priest, "with this difference, that they asked blood, and that I desired to give a free education to the children of the poor;" and he ended by recalling to his judges the example of Socrates "in the first struggle for freedom to teach." "In that *cause célèbre* by which Socrates fell," said Lacordaire, "he was evidently culpable against the gods, and in consequence against the laws of his country. Nevertheless, posterity, both pagan and Christian, has stigmatised his judges and accusers; and of all concerned have absolved only the culprit and the executioner,— the culprit, because he had failed to keep the laws of Athens, only in obedience to laws more elevated still; and the executioner, because he presented the cup to the victim with tears." When the elder defendant had thus proudly and plainly warned his judges of the possible fate before them, young Montalembert followed. He was in mourning, and his voice trembled as he alluded to "the voice so dear to me which lately sounded in this place." He was just twenty-one, and looked still younger than his age, his fresh, boyish, beardless face still preserving the first perfect outline and the evanescent bloom of youth. Everything in and about him tended to prepossess the friendly court before which he appeared; and when he justified himself in the following words, his youth, his simplicity, his beginning of eloquence, all must have pleaded for him :—

" I know that by myself I am nothing," said the young speaker; "I am but as a child; and I feel myself so young, so inexperienced, so obscure, that nothing less than the recollection of the great cause of which I am here the humble champion could encourage me. But I am happy in possessing a recollection of words pronounced for the same cause in this very place by my father. And I am sustained by the conviction that this is a question of life and

death for the majority of Frenchmen — for
twenty-five millions who hold the same religious faith as myself; and by the unanimous cry
of France for freedom of teaching ; and by the
written wishes of those fifteen thousand Frenchmen whose petition we have ourselves carried
to the other Chamber ; and by the rights of
thousands of families whose offspring are spring-
ing up in a region which arbitrary legislation
has made a desert ;—in one word, by the image
of a cruel past to atone for, and an invaluable
future to assert, and, above all, by the name I
bear—that name which is great as the world,
the name of Catholic. I have all these principles
to sustain me when I thus appear before you ;
and I require to remind myself of these great
arguments, not only to give me courage, but to
convince my judges that I have not been guided
in what I have done by any inspiration of
vanity, or any thirst for distinction. It is
sufficiently well known that the career on which
I have entered is not of a nature to satisfy
an ambition which seeks political honours and
places. The powers of the present age, both
in government and in opposition, are, by the
grace of Heaven, equally hostile to Catholics.
There is another ambition not less devouring,
perhaps not less culpable, which aspires to re-

putation, and which is content to buy that at any price : that, too, I disavow like the other. No one can be more conscious than I am of the disadvantages with which a precocious publicity surrounds youth, and none can fear them more. But there is still in the world something which is called faith—it is not dead in all minds; it is to this that I have early given my heart and my life. My life—a man's life—is always, and especially to-day, a poor thing enough; but this poor thing consecrated to a great and holy cause may grow with it; and when a man has made to such a cause the sacrifice of his future, I believe that he ought to shrink from none of its consequences, none of its dangers.

"It is in the strength of this conviction that I appear to-day for the first time in an assembly of men. I know too well that at my age one has neither antecedents nor experience; but at my age, as at every other, one has duties and hopes. I have determined, for my part, to be faithful to both."

We quote these words not so much as illustrating the early style of the future orator, but as manifesting the position he thus early took up. "It was thus," says M. Sainte-Beuve, " that M. de Montalembert, suddenly succeeding to the position of a peer on the very eve of the abolition of its hereditary character, made his *début* as an orator at the bar of the noble Chamber at the age of twenty-one, and in the position of defendant. But his youth, his ease and grace, the elegant precision of his style and diction, veiled this fact; and his judges were the first to forget that the speaker before them was one accused at their bar; they saw in him only the beginning of an orator. The entire Chamber listened with a surprise which was not without pleasure to the young man's bold self-justification, and, looking at its talent and grace alone, found in it first of all the highest promise of future public service. The House of Peers received this latest-born production of its hereditary right with the favour, and almost with the tenderness, which a mother has for the last of her children. From that day M. de Montalembert, though formally condemned, was borne in the very heart of the peerage—he was its Benjamin." Almost the same sentiment is expressed by the Duc de Broglie, who adds,— "The Chamber smiled at an eloquence so full of promise, as a grandsire smiles at the generous and mutinous vivacity of the last child of his race." The fervour and force and chivalrous courage of the young speaker stirred the noble blood of France, which was chilled in its veins by revolution and overthrow. Here was a proof that the chill was not for ever, that youth and enthusiasm could still rekindle the ancient fires. The defendants were sent from the bar of the Peers with a gentle reprimand, which was as good as an acquittal, and a mild fine of a hundred francs; and this defeat had, as was natural, all the effect of a victory.

CHAPTER V.

L'AVENIR CONTINUED, 1831.

THIS victory, however, though brilliant, was without results ; the young agitators, involved in a cloud of other occupations and excitements, had not leisure or patience to carry out the slow process of O'Connell's method, and get themselves re-tried, re-heard, and re-condemned, until their point was gained. On the contrary, having made this one remarkable assertion of their principles, they let it drop, or rather remitted it into private channels, into the hands of the Society for the Defence of Religious Liberty, and the tedious machinery of petitions and local agitations. We are not aware that any of the many French commentators upon the history of this brilliant year have noted the absence of the special circumstance which made O'Connell's agitation so successful—its perseverance, and perpetual repetition of the same attempt.

M. Cochin, in his able sketch,* remarks with a
certain astonished admiration upon the character of the brilliant but brief assault upon the
law, which was " so new, so unexpected, so
singular, and, in one word, so un-French."
" What," he says, " had led this young man, or
rather these two young men, to employ this
unusual method, this patient course of proceeding, which, making a formal commencement,
marches on step by step, mounting scientifically
to the assault, and conquering liberty with
patience and circumspection,—a course of proceeding, I repeat, so un-French ? "   Perhaps it
would be more to the instruction of the world
had the distinguished speaker inquired what
induced them to give it up.   Was it the natural impatience of their nation of a process so
gradual ? or was it the undiscriminating zeal of
youth, which knows no perspective, to which
all the objects it pursues are equally great and
equally practicable ? or was it simply the excitement of a combat more impassioned still,
which carried them away in spite of themselves,
and tore them from the practical point of freedom which they might have won, into the wild

* Le Comte de Montalembert : Discours prononcée le 1re
Avril 1870 à la Société Générale d'Education, par M. Augustin
Cochin, Membre de l'Institut.

pursuit of an ideal which they could never win?
Our own impression is, that they were moved
by all of these hindrances, but chiefly by the
latter.   For, indeed, that splendid abstraction of
religious liberty which the little army of the
' Avenir' hoped to conquer and realise, included
all lesser liberties, and made the individual
struggle unimportant.   The two young champions who had made so bold a beginning were
accordingly driven back into the larger and
more rapid stream : even Lacordaire, with all
his natural wisdom, was too much intoxicated
by the wild hope of that grand freedom of a
theocracy, which has charmed all pious imaginations since the beginning of time, to reflect
that the liberty to teach would have been much
easier to win ; and Montalembert, still younger
than he, full of romance and enthusiasm,
and with all the devotion of a disciple towards
the visionary Lamennais, the "master" whose
sway he was proud to acknowledge, could
scarcely be expected to sacrifice the ideal to
the practicable.   They did just enough, accordingly, to draw the eyes of France upon them,
to make an immense stir and commotion in
society, and to raise a question which, once
mooted, could sooner or later have but one
answer ; when they were swept away, as we

have said, by the wilder torrent, and, rushing after their chimera of an emancipated Church, let the possible victory drop for the moment out of their eager hands.

We are not of those who consider that this ideal of a self-governed Church, or, to adopt the words of its champions, a Church governed by God's laws alone, and unrestricted by the prudential enactments of men, is either a fanatical dream, or the invention of hypocritical ambition. We are certain, on the contrary, that not only to the three men whose brief but brilliant struggle we are endeavouring to set before the reader, but to many a humbler and less remarkable Christian, this ideal theocracy has been the highest and most beautiful vision which imagination could conceive. If we are compelled to add that it has never been successfully realised, this is no more than we are obliged to say of every high ideal ever conceived by man. Perhaps the conditions of human nature are such that it never will be realised; but yet the mind which cannot recognise the beauty and nobility of this hope is wanting in something, and does as much injustice to its own higher part as to the devout souls .at whom it sneers. A Church—who can doubt— which should be independent of all the coarser inducements of ambition ; which should be free to use every faculty for the advantage and succour of man ; which, poor itself, should be the natural champion of the poor ; which, free itself, should be the natural defender of all liberty ; which, acting on God's laws, and not on man's, should be the same everywhere, awful to the evil-doer, tender to the penitent, making religion a reality and not a form, and enlightening men everywhere as to their true interests, their wisest way,—who can doubt, we repeat, that such a Church, ideally pure, honest, and disinterested, would be the greatest benefactor the world ever saw ? And this was what their Church of the future appeared in the eyes of Lamennais, Lacordaire, and Montalembert. This was what, through the mists of distance, through the generous glamour of imagination, the Church in Ireland, poor and persecuted, but ever patriotic, maintaining in the midst of the most debasing poverty a certain spiritual standard of good and evil, and even a certain power of intellectual stimulation, appeared to them. Not only is the human interest of the situation entirely lost to those who refuse to acknowledge this real and most vivid hope and conviction, but life itself, and our own minds, are so much the poorer and duller from an inability to understand this variety of feeling. To these men the Church was the greatest of all agencies, and religion the highest of all influences; and the thought that such a power, so divinely adapted for all man's necessities, should be limited by frivolous bonds of local manufacture—should have its lips closed by a foolish edict—should be compelled to accept rulers chosen upon an altogether different principle from that of its foundation—should be stopped in its natural activity here, and forced there to do what it would not,—was altogether revolting and terrible to their minds. It is impossible to form any true idea of the subject of this memoir without fully identifying this fundamental principle. To him the idea of a secular statesman regulating the Church, excited the same flush of painful indignation which a soldier feels when he sees (as has been so often unhappily the case of recent days) the council of his generals thrown into confusion by the arbitrary interference of an ignorant civilian. Few men refuse to sympathise with the fury and indignation roused in the latter case; but in the former the world smiles or sneers at the sacerdotal pretension. Yet Montalembert, for one, was no sacerdotal devotee; his conflicts through life were as much with priests as with laymen. He was no worshipper of the priesthood; but he was a worshipper of the ideal Church; and this worship, and vision, and hope transported his soul.

While the foreground of the picture is occupied by the episode of the school, and the romantic and brilliant defence of the volunteer schoolmasters before the House of Peers, the background is filled up with a host of lesser activities. The Revolution of July had not passed over without some lawless consequences. In the very beginning of the year 1831, a funeral service in the beautiful church of Saint-Germain l'Auxerrois, on the anniversary of the murder of the Duc de Berry, was made the occasion of a great demonstration by the crowd against the Legitimists, and still more, as the Catholic party believed, against religion. This boiling over of the worst revolutionary feeling, that evil sediment which is in all popular ebullitions, and which had been wonderfully restrained and kept in check at the moment of revolution itself, took the vile form of an assault upon the church of Saint-Germain, which was seriously injured, crosses being in some cases pulled down from the walls and trampled under foot by the mob. At the same time the archbishop's palace was sacked, and almost destroyed. To make this outrage still more impressive, so far as young Montalembert was concerned, he himself was in arms, with his company of National Guards, posted at a point where they were totally unrequired, and hearing in the distance the tumult of destruction which they were not permitted to stop. A few years later he spoke in his place in the House of Peers of this riot, with a force of suppressed feeling extremely natural in the circumstances. " For my part," he said, " I can neither think of it nor talk of it calmly ; for I have still upon my heart the recollection of having been detained ten hours under arms, in the midst of twenty thousand bayonets equally unused, and detained far from the scene of the crime, while the waves of the Seine carried past us fragments of ruin from the archiepiscopal palace, bearing witness to the shame and impotence of society in these evil days." There can be little wonder that the young man's indignation exceeded all bounds at such a moment and under such circumstances. He poured it forth, glowing and flaming like the lava from a volcano, in the pages of the ' Avenir,' lamenting, not only in the interests of religion, but in those of outraged liberty, the insult thus done to the symbols of Christian faith. This article, which appeared on the 19th of February, six days after the riot, is entitled

" La Croix," and in it he pours forth the passion of his heart :—

" If there was ever a legitimate cause of sorrow, it is that which has seized our hearts in these days of anguish. We have not only to deplore, like some, that liberty, the name of which has been prostituted to cover the most revolting excesses; we have not only, like others, to strike our brows against the stones of our profaned altars—both these griefs are united in our grief; we are constrained to share all the complaints, all the groans, which recent events have torn from both parties; and who could be surprised if our souls should sink under the weight of this complication of evils and injuries? We had dreamt of a sublime alliance—this dream had become our life, we abandoned ourselves to it with the enthusiasm of young and fervent faith. We marched in the midst of darkness and in thorny ways, murmuring without cease two sacred names, and finding in these two names a consolation in all our weariness, an answer to all enmities, a remedy for all our sinkings of heart. These two names have been outraged, that sacred alliance has been thrown into the dust, this dream has ended, and we awake in the midst of the orgies of a sacrilegious people.

The future in which our souls dwelt, where our eyes sought a vivifying light, is veiled over; the powerful breath which inspired us with faith and courage is no longer anything but a faint sigh, which seems dying away. We lived by right of an immortal thought, and we have fallen into the arms of a mortal despair."

After this exordium, he addresses the two parties whose antagonism had brought on this assault upon the religion which embraced both, and had neither part nor lot in their quarrels.

"Men of the past," he cries, "how long will you remain faithful to this madness? how long will you persist in uniting that which God has put asunder, an eternal kingdom with one that passes away? When will you cease to betray the noble affections of your heart by an alliance which equally ruins both causes which are dear to you? It has been your doing: you have fastened your *fleur-de-lis* to a crucifix, and the people have protested against the union by a sacrilege.

"And to the others we say: 'Men of power, dare you still lull yourselves in the hope that this power will be able to save your faith? dare you confide to it the destinies of the Church of

God, give up to it the choice of her pastors, and sell the tribute of your prayers to that authority which, with sixty thousand bayonets under its orders, has permitted churches to be destroyed, and has left the most sacred signs of that worship, of which you proclaim yourself the defenders, to be dragged through the mud and thrown into the stream.'"

This glowing protest was followed by another appeal, an address to the Royalist party, whose alliance was so great a danger for the Church, yet who were as profoundly opposed as the men of July to the politics and mission of the 'Avenir.' It is very evident that the heart of the young writer was moved towards this party, which included so large a proportion of his own class, even when his opinions were most strongly against them ; and it was, we believe, partly as a counterpoise to an article of excessive rigour against the Royalist party, written by Lamennais, that this warm and eloquent appeal, " À ceux qui aiment ce qui fut," was published. It is an anxious remonstrance against the fatal practice common to the higher classes of France, and apparently to the classes most distinguished by education and refinement, wherever democracy rules supreme, of withdrawing from all share in the political life of their country, and in pride or in sullenness leaving the mob to rule by themselves. The address with which it begins has something singularly and touchingly personal in it, like the address of one brother to another, and shows the generous and poetic soul of the young writer as in a glass.

" We who are new to public life and to the conflicts which have absorbed your existence, we do not represent ourselves to you as partisans of your political faith, or neophytes of that worship of legitimate kings which you profess, without making any account of the legitimacy of nations; but we say in simplicity and good faith—if you but knew how much we respect the unfortunate love, how much we venerate the long enthusiasm of your fidelity, and how, above all, the common faith which unites us calls forth our sympathy, you would regret the dissensions which separate us, you would recognise in us children of the same father—Christians to whom it is grievous not to be united with other Christians in all their thoughts, and who long to gather all together in a unity higher than that which can be dissolved by the events of earth.

" We feel none of this sympathy, God knows,

for the regrets of courtiers, the disappointment
of officials, the mortifications of self-love or
ambition which produce nothing more than
conspiracies of the drawing-room and miserable
petty conflicts.   But we feel a sympathy strong
and deep for the disinterested attachment of
those provincial Royalists, of those rural populations which have never seen the Court, which
have received nothing from it, which have
gained nothing by its return, and lost nothing
by its fall.   The former, very much more closely
linked to the ancient dynasty and involved in
its faults, have been the first to march under
the new banner; the latter have remained unshaken in their affection, in the sadness of their
regret, in the worship of that hereditary belief
which they cherish as a holy patrimony.   We
respect them, and we have had need of all our
faith in the eternal designs of God, we have had
need of all the awe inspired by those terrible
chastisements with which he strikes kings and
peoples, to keep us from being drawn by too
warm a sentiment towards men of such stain-
less honour.   Governed, however, by a thought
which is higher than all thrones, and with our
eyes fixed upon the future, which God permits
us to see in glimpses, we do not share their
regrets, but we are profoundly touched by

them ; we do not live under the empire of their
loves and recollections, but we bow ourselves
before their self-devotion ; for wherever there is
self-devotion there is faith, and wherever there
is faith there is the breath of God."

This preface shows how nearly the young man,
preux chevalier and champion of the unfortunate, he who hated victorious causes, had been led
away by his chivalrous sympathy for the fallen
into the ranks of the absolutist party—a position
in which he could not have found rest for a
moment. But interesting as this is personally,
it is not more so than the patriotic wisdom of
his hot young pleading with this party, to come
out of its sullen or contemptuous seclusion,
and take its just and constitutional part in the
conduct of the nation.

"You possess" (he says) "half of the soil of
France ; by your numbers, by your faith, by
your virtues, even by your wealth, you are invincible. How do you dare then to remain
longer apart from the struggles which decide
day by day the dearest interests of your
country ? While you await the time when
you can expose your lives for her on the field
of battle, why do you shrink from the duties

of peaceful and free citizens ? Royalists, nobles of France, landed gentlemen, we exhort you formally; make use of the innumerable advantages of your position, make use of the legitimate influence which belong to you over the masses. Confess frankly those opinions of which it is attempted to make a crime, and which legislative restriction endeavours in vain to annul. Attach to yourselves once more, by your disinterestedness, by your tenderness, by your devotion to the general interest, the populations which surround you. Do not misunderstand the double popularity to which you are called—the powerful popularity of official disfavour and the holy popularity of virtue.

" Enter then with courage and confidence into public life. Hasten to enroll yourselves in the ranks of the National Guard ; ask arms from the country, and swear not to lay them down when your God is insulted. Fulfil zealously the sacred duty of electors, and give to the country representatives who will understand the true union of order and freedom. Called to share in the national sovereignty, make use of it with that seriousness and conscience which France demands of you. Do, in a word, what your fathers did—make with us and with all men of good faith, who seriously love liberty, *a league for the public good*, upon which at once the attacks of impiety and the evil snares of power will fall. Throw the weight of your virtues into the balance when God weighs the destinies of the country, and suffer no longer the baseness of a ruffian or the power of a speculator to precipitate it into the dust."

It would have been well for France if all the better and purer spirits, whose devotion to a dead cause have made them useless for her service, would have taken these wise words— almost too wise to have come from a brain of one-and-twenty—to heart. Unfortunately they have never done so; and perhaps the most fatal particular in all the evils brought about by her many revolutions is, that one detachment after another of her best and wisest has been paralysed and laid aside, to look on while their inferiors both in mind and morals did the public work and debased the national character. At this very moment, when all the elements are in confusion, and no one knows which will come uppermost, there is nothing more discouraging to a patriotic Frenchman than the consciousness of that voiceless crowd which stands aside looking on and taking no share in whatever is done in the country, leaving the scum to come uppermost and have its way. The very existence of this dumb passive mass, which neither votes nor speaks, in the midst of all the agitations around, is a wonderful fact. It was but to one portion of this—a portion kept silent by its sympathies with the past, and not by mere apathy—that Montalembert made his impassioned appeal; but the appeal might be extended in its application, and even heightened in its entreaties, were there any such voice as his to sound it now into the ear of the country which he loved to his last breath.

We will quote but one other fragment from these glowing pages of the 'Avenir.' The articles on Poland, of which there are three or four, are so many poems, lyrics of an enthusiasm which might sound extravagant if it were not so tuneful and so full of unbounded and most generous sympathy for valour and misfortune. These lyrical outbursts, however, we leave to be sought out by those who are still (if such remain), or have been, enthusiasts for Poland. But there is a short article, entitled "La Foi," also from the 'Avenir,' strangest composition for a newspaper—a lofty, melancholy, half-inspired strain, which reads like an echo of something proclaimed to an awe-stricken people by a primitive prophet — from which we will quote an impressive picture of that world without faith which was, the writer sadly felt, before his eyes as he wrote. Once more the political party, which professed itself Christian, shared, with the avowedly profane, the indignant and eloquent warning of this young monitor.

" A great void has been made in the heart of every individual and of every people ; and this void is heavy as a punishment, wearisome as a death-struggle. Driven about by the wind of their caprices upon the ocean of human misery, nations and men have closed their sails to one breath only, and that is the breath of God. There is no more union among them, no self-surrender, no more tender affections, no more heartfelt faith ; a dull defiance has replaced all this, and its icy empire is shared only by derision and bitterness. Kings and great men, who were the first to undermine the soil of the Christian world, have felt that soil tremble beneath them, and have so fallen into contempt and impotence that the day of their funeral will be for them a day of mercy. The people, enriched only for a moment by the fall of its masters, no longer knows with what intention it broke their yoke, and now gazes with consternation upon the earth, which remains barren under its victory, and upon the heaven, which it does not understand. Seated between the tomb of his fathers, whom he has disowned, and the cradle of his children, for whom he feels only a bitter pity, man is no more than a melancholy puppet, condemned to play I know not what lugubrious comedy before I know not what icy spectators.

"Alas! and it is not only in the hearts of the impious and of the children of perdition that the divine breath is extinct—that the heavenly life is at its last sigh. The children of God, what are they doing? . . . Worshippers of the past, where is that faith which your fathers found everywhere, and which inspired all their self-devotion, which presided over all their affections, which mingled itself with their whole life? Is it this which governs all your passions, which reigns over all your attachments—is it this which is the root of all your hopes? . . . No; deaf to the voice of Him who came into the world alone and without human alliance, they are led away by their foolish passions, to seek a god, according to their fancy, under the folds of some royal mantle, or within the circlet of a mortal crown. . . . They believe with blind faith in the immortal power of a family, in the miraculous destiny of a child, in the terrible punishment of their enemies; but tell them that God is there in the midst of those crumbling thrones, of this volcanic agitation of peoples, in this martyrdom of a nation of heroes; tell them that it is His hand which regulates the vast field of revolutions, and that He gathers all His creatures thus for the work of His glory; tell them so, and they will shake off the dust from their feet against you—they will retire from you, they will fly into solitude, into idleness. For what reason, oh my God?—to forget and to betray Thee!

"There is no more life in the world; the thought of God, which has been everywhere banished, has carried with it everywhere duration, truth, and life. For the personal affections, as for political attachments, there is no longer a sacred sanction, and no longer a future. Where is the tie which has not been broken? Where is the cause which is not distrusted? Where is the principle which reigns as a master over a single soul? An indescribable giddiness has seized upon men—no one knows where he is going, no one wishes to go where his fate urges him. They lie, they heap oath upon oath; but all their vain words, in which God is not once named, are quickly effaced from the recollection of men.　Just enough of memory is left to them to know themselves perjured."

It is thus that the young agitator, the young polemic, the youth who at the same moment was playing the curious little episode of his schoolmastership, and was presently to defend that daring Quixotism before his peers—it was thus he wrote in one of those sad moments of inspiration which belong to young genius.　He was sad ; his heart was torn for his country, and for that absence of all concern for the better part which was her melancholy characteristic ; and yet at the same time—as we see in a hundred ways—even while he uttered these melancholy fulminations, he was full of hope and light-heartedness, doing his work with a cheerful enthusiasm which never forsook him, and expecting everything that was good and joyful for his people and his faith.　This practical paradox is always possible to youth ; and it was happily possible to his vigorous and vivacious spirit at all times of his life, even when youth was long past.　But in the mean time youth breathes in all he does and says, even in the unmeasured force of his exultation and despair, his sense of immense downfall and his certainty of success to come.　No compromises were possible to him. What he said, he said with all his heart, throwing himself into it with *abandon* and unreserve, with absolute earnestness and faith.

At the same time other work than that of simple journalists occupied the conductors of the 'Avenir.' The Society for the Defence of Religious Liberty was as active as the newspaper which was its organ. Montalembert announces in his journal that he was himself in communication with twenty-two departments, and the energetic propagandism which they carried on involved many journeys through France for the formation of local societies and the encouragement of new disciples. " The means of communication, both personal and by post," he says at a later period, " were much more difficult than now ; there were neither railways nor telegraphs ; and in our propagandist journeys we took three days and three nights to go, in execrable diligences, from Paris to Lyons." Some of these journeys are amusingly referred to in the letters of Lacordaire, where he throws many a friendly gibe at his friend's dainty personal habits—for Montalembert in this particular was English in all his ways, indulging in those perpetual baths and ablutions which puzzle the true Continental soul ; and insisted upon making himself fresh and clean and neat on his arrival at a new place, whatever might be the hour or the circumstances. This delightful peculiarity made his friend smile, and he upbraids him lovingly with "tes toilettes de deux heures;" which, however, after a diligence-journey of three days and three nights, every Englishman will sympathise in. All this movement and activity was life and joy to Montalembert. In the beginning of 1831 he had the great grief of losing one of the friends of his boyhood, Gustave Lesmarcis, who died after a long illness at Nice, and, as it happened, on the very day when Montalembert had sadly visited and gazed with many recollections at the closed windows of his house at Conflans. But even under this blow his work supported him. "Now that I am no longer idle, I can bear anything," he says. His occupations, too, threw him into the midst of a little crowd of men of congenial enthusiasm, who thought and felt as he did, and upon whose imaginations the beautiful dream of a free Church had made a similar impression. Enthusiasm of this kind, when real, is perhaps the most beautiful and ardent of all enthusiasm, especially as manifested by the young laymen, who could derive no personal advantage of any kind from the Church's emancipation, and whose disinterested glow of zeal, and eagerness for the freedom of religion, had all the grace and warmth of patriotism, with a certain visionary and pure flame added to it, more tender and elevating than patriotism itself.

> "Good was it in that time to be alive,
> But to be young was very heaven:"

this is the spirit of the words in which, going back with happy sadness into his own recollections, Montalembert draws for us with his own hand the picture of this period—the year of the 'Avenir':—

"I will be pardoned for dwelling upon the events of this year, which were so memorable for us. There is no man, however obscure and little worth his life may have been, who does not at the end of his days feel himself drawn by an irresistible current towards the moment when the first fire of enthusiasm awoke his soul and trembled on his lips; there are none who do not breathe with a sort of intoxication the perfume of their recollections, and who do not feel themselves tempted to boast beyond measure of their charm and brilliancy. Happy and sad days, we say to ourselves—days devoured by work and passion, days such as one sees but once in one's life! I do not fear to exaggerate the value and the intensity of those struggles for the essential principles in question, which decided the attitude of Catholics in France and elsewhere from the Revolution of July to the time of the Second Empire. The present generation can form little idea of the strong and generous passions which then inflamed all hearts. . . . What life there was in the soul! what fervour in the intelligence! what disinterested worship of the flag, the cause! how many deep and fruitful furrows were made in the young hearts of the time by an idea, by an act of self-devotion, by a great example, by an instance of faith or of courage! . . . To understand the pure and disinterested enthusiasm which then burst forth in the parsonages of the young clergy, and in certain groups of frank and noble young men, one must have lived in these times, read in their eyes, received their confidences, grasped their tremulous hands, and contracted in the heat of the combat ties which death alone could break."

The same sentiment is also expressed by Lacordaire. "However cruel Time may be," he says, "it can take nothing from the happiness of the year which is just over, and which will remain in my heart for ever like a virgin newly dead."

It was their year of romance, the blossom of more than one life, to which other blossom was denied. Lamennais, a man who does not seem to have been susceptible to the more vulgar attractions of ecclesiastical ambition, whose fame was *pur et simple*, without either bishop's mitre or cardinal's hat in prospect, rose and expanded with this sudden access of ambition for his Church; bursting as it were into full flower of hope, after long years of vague verdure and indefinite growth. Lacordaire, who beneath his exuberance of imagination and eloquence hid all the passion of a reserved and self-concentrated nature, had let himself go upon the delightful current of enthusiasm, opening for once in his life the very floodgates, and pouring himself forth with that conscious effusion and self-forgetfulness which in its very fulness grows more full, breaking every boundary in the delicious sense of *abandon* which is so difficult to it on ordinary occasions. Montalembert's position was different; for in him the material had been all ready waiting the first strong influence which should seize it; and the facts which determined the nature of this influence were, so far as it is permissible to use such words, entirely fortuitous. But all the more eager was this first application of his abstract enthusiasm to real work, an ardent and tumultuous stream, carrying all before it.

Around these three were a little crowd of men, chiefly young, who had escaped out of the bare and hard monotony of the secular schools, that unlovely level of cynicism and profaneness which, whatever its opinions may be, revolts every sensitive mind; or, on the other hand, out of the ecclesiastical seminaries, with their narrow horizons, and that routine of observance which lies heavy upon the young priest, just as the routine of non-observance disgusts the young layman. Out of all these different burdens, out of the monotonous life which brought nothing but disappointment, where even revolution changed little in the people, and even misfortune mended little in a king, this group of lives burst into sudden flower. The principle, which was their life and bond of union, was something altogether new, though old as Christianity; and never was there a time which had more need of a new hope, never time more painfully conscious of wanting some legitimate and undebased link with the past. And this new thing was a something yet untried—a power which had never had fair-play; most probably, nay, most certainly, as they all felt, it was the one panacea neglected all this time, which might heal the world. As they rushed about all over the country, spreading the news of it, finding everywhere a fit audience, often few but always worthy, what wonder if their hearts burned within them more and more, and if their confidence grew day by day in this infallible remedy which they had discovered, and which was to heal all ills? Outside of the little band many of the best minds of France stood curious, looking on, touched by the enthusiasm, prepossessed by the genius employed on this new crusade, wondering what it was all to come to, and admiring though they gave no adherence. Victor Cousin might denounce them as *gens de la Sacristie*, but Victor Hugo gazed at them with sympathetic attention, dreaming of a world regenerated by Catholicism; and was not the *Sacristie* itself part of the Church, and the reproach such as might be taken up proudly, and in very scorn of scorn made into a distinction? Those who stood aloof from them, those who vilified them, were, it seemed to these enthusiasts, the commonplace mass both of people and priests, who were unable to understand the height of their hopes, or the magnanimous and generous character of their enterprise. Vulgar statesmen, who feared ecclesiastical influence above all things; clergy who trembled for the poor remnant of position and provision which was still left to them; and those profane masses who tore down the cross from the church wall, and sacked houses, and destroyed whatever they could find to destroy,—such were their enemies: while all that was noblest and purest in the Church of the past—all that was great, generous, and expansive in the Church of the future, was on their side; or so at least they thought. And more and more, as that vulgar opposition grew hotter, their ideal became dearer to them—the ideal of the Church separated for ever from all the vile ties which bound her to the side of the great, which tempted her to ambition and worldly wants and wishes— divinely poor, divinely free, going about doing good like her Master, having, like Him, perhaps, no place to lay her head, yet ministered to by angels, protected by God, delivering man. We do not hesitate to say that it was a noble and beautiful dream. However little we may agree with them, however impracticable the idea may seem to us, and however history may pronounce against it, no sympathetic mind can ever look on without a thrill of admiration and fellow- feeling at such an enterprise. It could not but fail; but those who believed in its possibility proved themselves by so doing to be men of a heroic strain.

And the leaders who were so united in work were at the same time brethren, and more than brethren, in heart. They lived in the same house, making a family of themselves under the genial fatherhood of Lamennais, and establishing a home and centre to which all sympathies naturally came, and which overflowed with the lively stir of business, and the intimate and loving intercourse of youthful friendship. There is a glimpse of this common dwelling-place in one of the letters addressed by Lacordaire to his friend while absent on one of the many journeys of the *Agence.* "We have left the Rue de l'Université," he writes ; "there was no longer anything to keep us there—at least there was nothing to keep me, as you were there no longer. We are now at No. 98 Rue de Vaugirard. It is a pleasant house. Besides the entrance court there is another large gravelled court at the side, and a good garden, in which we shall take our walks. M. Feli (the diminutive of Felicité, by which name all his disciples addressed Lamennais) occupies the ground-floor to the left. The chapel is above his rooms, and by the side of it two pleasant apartments for M. Gerbet and M. Combalot. Above them,

on the second floor, nobody lives at present.
On the third floor, on the left of the court, is
my room, which has two large windows commanding an immense view from the hills of
Montmartre to the Castle of Meudon, and even
further off, taking in St Sulpice, l'Abbaye, the
Arc de Triomphe, the Invalides—while close by
is the garden of the house, which fills in the
foreground as if it had been made for that alone.
This, however, is not the best of my apartment.   It is entered by a door at the end of the
corridor, but there is another door which admits
to a charming room, which I have taken possession of for you.   Thus we shall be together.
If I should have chosen wrongly for you, and
you would rather not have a room so close to
your friend, the place must remain vacant.   I
speak of the house, and not of the heart."

" Return quick, my dear friend, return quick,"
he adds a few days later.   " We need you, and
I can no longer live without you.   Every day I
go into your room, which is beside mine, to open
the window and put it in order, as if you
were already there.   But even friendship cannot
create what does not exist.   I have been in low
spirits these few days because of our change.
How good it would be to die in the place where
one was born, without ever leaving the same

roof ! but there are few so happy in this world,
and even the rich are wanderers (vagabonds)
like others.   Palaces have ceased to be hereditary as well as cabins.   We are like those wood-
men who make themselves a hut at the foot of
a tree, and after having destroyed everything
around them, finish by cutting down the very
trunk against which they supported their heads,
before they leave the spot.   Let us make at least
an eternal friendship in the midst of this world,
where there is no longer anything durable and
unchanging.   Let our hearts be as the hearths
of our fathers.   My good René, I await your
coming; I entreat you not to linger on the
way.   How strange to take any pleasure in
being absent !   Besides, we want you.   .   .   .
We have scarcely enough spoons to eat our soup,
or beds to sleep in.   It is a bivouac."

Thus poor, sad, joyful, and busy, hoping
everything and possessing nothing, with no
support but work and friendship, and the high
ambition of serving their country, the little
band laboured and struggled, sometimes put to
sad straits, but never losing courage, and with a
certain lawlessness in their bold career which
must have afforded a gleam of pleasure at least
to the younger brethren of the dauntless party.
The 'Avenir,' indeed, throughout all its short

career, is more like a spiritual Quixote than an ordinary newspaper. It goes against every ill deed and ill doer in its way with a rush and fury which make the sober spectator giddy, flinging itself at the head of its adversary, rejecting all thoughts of expediency, maintaining a cause as superlative as that of any sacred majesty or Utopian republic, the cause of the absolute Best in a world full of compromises. The rights it claimed for the Church, and the impossible sacrifices which it promised in her name, raised for it enemies on every side, thick and many. The Church and the world equally erected themselves against so generous yet so rash a champion; for if the world was determined not to grant the absolute rights thus claimed, the Church was as little disposed to follow the beck of its self-appointed leaders, and give up even the poor remnant of revenue that was left to her, her morsel of bread, at its call.

While all the world thus rose in resistance to the counsels of the 'Avenir,' the resources of its little band began to be exhausted, and the moment grew nearer and nearer in which downfall must come. By what a singular and romantic expedient the end of this curious knight-errant of newspapers was made different from all other such conclusions, we can best explain in the words of that one of its editors whose good sense at this moment was most to be relied on, yet who, strangely enough, was the author of the rash suggestion which brought so much trouble upon all the band. It is Lacordaire who speaks :—

"At the same time," he says, after describing the origin and policy of the paper, " this movement had not a foundation sufficiently broad. It was too sudden and too ardent to sustain itself for a long period. To have a steady success, it is necessary that an enterprise should be deeply rooted in the spirit of the time. Although O'Connell had gone before us, he was in a great measure unknown to France; and we appeared to the clergy, to Government, to all parties, like a parcel of children, without ancestors and without posterity. Our undertaking was as the tempest coming from the desert, and not like the fruitful rain which refreshes the air and blesses the fields. It was necessary, then, after thirteen months of a daily combat, to think of retreat. Our funds were exhausted, our courage failing, our strength diminished even by the extravagance with which we had employed it. The same day when this resolution was taken, I went early to the room of M. de la Mennais, and showed him that we could not come to an end like this, but that we ought to go to Rome to justify our meaning, to submit our opinions to that tribunal, and to give, by this proceeding, such a proof of our sincerity and orthodoxy as would be always, whatever might happen, a blessing to us, and a weapon taken out of the hand of our enemies."

Enlightened by the wisdom of experience—that wisdom which never comes soon enough to stop a foolish enterprise—Lacordaire complains that Lamennais, who was twenty years his senior, and ought to have known better, did not make the least objection to this mad but most touching and simple reference to what the honest young priest considered an infallible tribunal of justice. But Lamennais was not one of the men who learn by experience, or who was ever likely to stop, by cold intervention of wisdom, a proposal so attractive. He accepted the idea at once, without pause or hesitation. "Yes," he said, "we must go to Rome." It was a course in accordance with all his own feelings; it was a brilliant and romantic way of escaping from the dead prose of failure; and it was, at the same time, a possible means of triumphing over all the petty oppositions and

enmities which they had encountered. It is
evident that the idea of a repulse from Rome
never entered into his mind. In his former
visit he had been received with nothing but
applauses. The sweetest of praise—that which
is bestowed by one's chief whom one half adores,
and who is the highest authority upon earth to
us—had been lavished upon him; and no doubt
Lamennais anticipated new triumphs, and that
his cause would be splendidly vindicated, and
he himself made triumphant over his enemies.
Montalembert was too young to make any opposition to such a proposal, and too enthusiastic
to do anything but embrace it with delight.
Accordingly, a last number of the 'Avenir'
was published, in which the purpose of the
editors to suspend the paper until they had
gone to Rome to seek sanction and authority for
its continuation, was announced " with pomp,"
as Lacordaire tells us; and the most curious
pilgrimage ever undertaken either in modern or
ancient days began. In the nineteenth century,
on the morning after a revolution, these three
modern Frenchmen, thorough men of their time,
set out accordingly, with a simplicity worthy
of the heroic ages, to seek approval of their
opinions and works from their spiritual head.
Neither from primitive Ireland nor romantic

Poland had such an expedition set forth. These two examples of faith and obedience had fighting enough on hand, and mixed motives, on which perhaps they could not, with a safe conscience, seek the Pope's blessing. But the Frenchmen did it, who were sprung of the most sceptical race on earth, and at one of its worst moments. It was reserved for them to give this extraordinary, *bizarre,* yet most touching proof of a faith as real as that which moved Saint Louis. In ancient days they would have gone with pilgrim staff and shoon, making the journey toilsomely and slowly ; but though they travelled instead in the quietest, most civilised, and commonplace manner, it was no less a pilgrimage. If they had done nothing more to prove their unworldliness, their generous unwisdom, trust, candour, and good faith, they must have demonstrated them now beyond all question. And of all the expeditions undertaken in this century, we doubt if there is one other as affecting, as remarkable, as simple, and strange. They went to their Pope with that absolute realisation of their relationship to him as children to their father, which is so confusing to the unimaginative soul. They took it for a fact, this theory, this matter of abstract belief, and acted upon it, putting all ordinary mortals, who keep facts and theories apart in their distinct places, into such a ferment of embarrassment and bewilderment as fortunately occurs but seldom, even in the wonderful world of Rome.

CHAPTER VI.

DOWNFALL.

IT is evident that this extraordinary expedition was undertaken with very little fear of its results. The conductors of the 'Avenir' had so much faith in their principles and in the supreme authority to whom they referred their cause, that they went sure not only of a just judgment but of a triumphant vindication. They felt, as David did when he referred his cause to God, that the Vicar of Christ would bring out their righteousness as the noonday. From mocking Paris, full then as now of gaiety and trifling and laughter, where many scoffed at them and all wondered, they went out, holding their heads high in the primitive certainty of their faith. They took their " devout imagination," their impossible ideal, without any misgivings, from that world of levity into the graver centre of astute policy and traditionary wisdom. And they went to ask the Head of the Church to commit himself, to sanction a new and revolutionary movement, to bless the very banners of revolt, and acknowledge as pioneers of his army the ecclesiastical Ishmaels who had carried fire and flame everywhere during their brief career. The looker-on cannot but smile at an expedition so unlikely; but it was real as life and death to the pilgrims who undertook it, and who, in their conviction of the justice of their cause, were for the moment absolutely without fear.

The 'Avenir' came to an end in November 1831 ; and immediately after, "we set out," says Lacordaire—"M. de la Mennais, M. de Montalembert, and I—like three soldiers worn out by war, seeking rest from their combats under the paternal roof." The two elder pilgrims arrived in Rome on the eve of the new year; but Montalembert, who was now making his first visit to Italy, travelled less directly, and we find him in December in Florence, where he formed one of his sudden but devoted friendships with the young Albert de la Ferronays, son of Count de la Ferronays, ambassador at Rome under Charles X., who had resigned his post after the Revolution of July, and who, like so many other noble Legitimists, had been obliged to fall back upon the remains of a fortune much diminished by the first Revolution, and continued in an honourable exile, poor, pious, and irreproachable, in the country to which he had been sent as representative of France. It is at this point that the subject of this memoir enters into one of the most delicate and exquisite pictures ever drawn,—a narrative in which the life of a real family is set fully and frankly before us, without ever once conveying to the reader a sense of sacred privacy invaded or undue confidence given. The 'Recit d'une Sœur' is too well known to require any praise or any description here. It is unique in literature. It is a romance more detailed and more effusive than fiction, a love-story as pure as ever maiden dreamed, a tale in which the most private incidents of life are recorded without the smallest breach of that modesty which is indispensable to honourable existence. It throws, at the same time, into the most lovable and attractive light, the virtues and excellences of that *vieille noblesse* which has unfortunately lost the influence it ought to have had in France, but which retains so much that is noblest and purest and most admirable in human character, and has produced some of the most delightful individual men and women ever brought into the world.

The new friend of Montalembert, the hero of this beautiful book, Albert de la Ferronays, was not a man calculated for the rougher work of the world. He was one of those spotless and tender souls, " most gentle, most unfortunate," to whom Providence makes up for the early death which awaits them by giving them in their lifetime, heaped up and running over, the gift of universal love and sympathy. He was at Florence with M. Rio, the future historian of Christian art, when young Montalembert, as usual seeing and describing everything, arrived in Florence. The two youths were nearly the same age, and had many sentiments in common. Albert had been making a tour through Tuscany, visiting with Rio the most interesting points in that lovely country, and those which were most distinguished by historical and religious recollections; and had paused to make a " retreat " at Florence in all the tender enthusiasm of that youthful piety which is so much more angelic, if often perhaps less real, than piety at any other age; and which had, no doubt, been warmed and strengthened by the sight of many a church and castle and village made memorable by saintly legends. The three travellers passed some time together in Florence; and it was here probably, under the influence and teaching of M. Rio, that the first strong impulse towards religious art, and appreciation of its beauty and meaning, came to Montalembert. They went to Rome together, according to Madame Craven, in January 1832, though from the recollections of M. Rio, as published in his Epilogue to 'l'Art Chrétien,' he and Albert would seem to have followed and not accompanied their common friend.

Lacordaire and Lamennais had reached Rome on the last day of 1831, and there Montalembert rejoined them. From the first moment of their entrance into that centre of all their hopes, a change is evident in the very atmosphere surrounding the three pilgrims. A sombre cloud immediately enveloped their life. Out of the free air and the sunshine the two priests plunged at once into chill and shadow. Their younger companion had all the advantages of his greater youth, his rank, and his condition of layman to sustain him; but he too felt the difference. The shade of ecclesiastical Rome—calm, patient, swallowing up enthusiasm, a place not of the present, in which the affairs of the passing day seem impertinences—came over them all at once, chilling the very blood in their excited veins, thrusting thoughts upon them which had never intruded their disagreeable presence before. The terrible possibility of disappointment—a possibility unforeseen and unregarded hitherto—came all at once upon them. They had come out of a fever of work, endless exertion, and excitement, into absolute quiet and repose. They had come from the company of men who thought like themselves—and of men who thought exactly the reverse, yet so far respected and feared their effort as to combat it hotly—into the calm and indifference of a community which knew little about them, and cared less. The very greatness of the hope which had brought them here gave bitterness to the mortification with which they found themselves not even assailed or condemned, but passed over without notice. It was such a trial as few men have to bear, and it came upon them with so little preparation that the hardship was doubled. The curious stillness that followed their arrival in Rome strikes the reader with a sense of uneasiness and suspense and coming storm, as does the hush before a tempest. No doubt they tried to say to themselves that here was the moment of peace they had longed for; that the wearied soldiers were resting in their father's house : and many a specious piece of self-argument besides to convince themselves

that all was well and going well; but this is
only one of the bitterest forms of unacknow-
ledged downfall, and soon they were unable to
lull themselves into quiet even by such flattering thoughts.

Their first step in Rome had been to visit
some of the old friends of Lamennais, who
during his previous residence there had received
him as a saint, almost as a god; but these were
the days when his portrait hung in Leo XII.'s
cabinet, and every voice was in his favour.
The *accueil très réservé* which their old acquaintances gave would seem to have been the
first thing which threw chill enlightenment
upon the mind of Lacordaire, who, as became
his nature, was the first to discover the mistake
they had made.   Lamennais either could not or
would not perceive the tacit evidences of Papal
displeasure expressed by the cold looks of his
friends and the neglect shown of his presence.
But Lacordaire, whose *amour propre* was not so
deeply concerned, perceived it at once.   The
change of the place had changed the position
altogether.   In Paris, Montalembert and Lacordaire had already gained notoriety, and, though
not equal in fame to their master, were still
individually notable—first actors in the feverish
little drama.   In Rome these two young men

were in a great degree reduced to the *rôle* of spectators. They were young, and they were nameless, while Lamennais was recognised as a personage worthy of censure, as he had once been worthy of applause. This spectator-position no doubt quickened the sight, naturally clear, penetrating, and practical, of Lacordaire. Other influences too affected him. It was his first visit to Rome, and that fact of itself impressed his mind deeply. "He, a journalist and bourgeois of 1830," says Montalembert, " a democrat in all his opinions, perceived at the first glance not only the inviolable majesty of the supreme pontificate, but its difficulties, its long and patient plans, and the policy which was indispensable in managing men and things." In short, he perceived that to call upon an old, majestic, world-ruling authority, compelled to consider the interest of all Christendom, and to observe the traditionary policy of centuries, to approve and adopt a bran-new, untried, political movement, was at once hopeless and absurd. In taking this view he made himself the representative of that large body of reasonable men, not only in the Roman communion, but in all others, who, finding it impossible to carry the authority of their Church with them in secondary points, have tacitly abandoned their polemical position, and decided upon keeping their personal opinions to themselves, rather than give up the immense moral support of that Church in their attempt to teach and elevate their fellow-creatures. This was the position taken up by Lacordaire. He had been the first to recommend this step; he was the first to see its futility and foolishness; and at the same time he had moral courage enough to be the first to suggest its abandonment, and the relegation into safe silence of all the impracticable absolutism of their rash and impetuous claims.

Lamennais was a man of different nature, different views, the representative of a totally different class. His circumstances, too, were different. He had won just fame by the exertions of his past life, and he had committed himself and his reputation to the issue of this enterprise. If he failed and was condemned, who in the Roman world would think of the humble young priest, Henri Lacordaire, or of the enthusiast-boy, Charles de Montalembert? They were but as children, involved, but lightly involved, in the failure of a father. Their future was not compromised, nor their life stultified. Even with Lacordaire, to whom as a priest the complication was more serious, the 'Avenir' and all its rash chivalry might be swept away, and yet he might survive. It might pass absolutely from the face of the earth, and be as if it had never been, and the worst reproach to which he could be liable would be that his zeal had outrun his discretion, a fault easily excused in a young man. But Lamennais was fifty, a power in the Church, with an immense reputation, and the eyes of many upon him. He was past the age when men, foiled in one enterprise, can lightly or cheerfully take up another; and having once taken such a step, he could not retire unnoticed. Withdrawal, if a more dignified proceeding personally, would have been, so far as the public were concerned, as bad as condemnation. Besides all this, there had happened to him a thing which sometimes befalls a calm thinker unawares, after years engaged in philosophical speculations and deliberations, which have never roused his soul into excitement—he had become possessed by something more mighty than the highest authority, by a strong and deep personal conviction, a determined and absolute sense that he was right, though heaven and earth should pronounce against him. This fact carried him into an entirely different atmosphere from that of his companions. Clearly his only hope, the only chance of escape for him, the sole means of preserving his allegiance as a Catholic, lay in the possibility of persuading, praying, insisting, forcing the Papal authority to agree with him. If this could not be done, what was the abyss that darkly opened before his feet, what the ruin that threatened him? Men in this state of feeling are like stars broken loose from their orbits, if stars ever could break loose. If they cannot be held by some subtle power of attraction, the only course possible to them is to crash wildly through space, wounded and wounding, till they drop into the unfathomable depths below. The position is tragical, pitiful, terrible in its hopelessness; and Lamennais's aspect during this interval of suspense is not so much that of a man anxiously hoping for a favourable result, as of one possessed by the determination of despair to procure at all hazards the sentence which alone could keep his life in harmony with itself.

We are obliged to insist upon those two different attitudes of his companions, in order to show the reader the position which young Montalembert occupied between them, with his heart torn asunder, loved and trusted and argued with by both — preaching hope to one and patience to the other, and getting wounded on both sides as peacemakers generally do. He was too candid and reasonable even now not to perceive the wisdom of Lacordaire's better judgment ; but he was warmly attached to his "Master," and quite incapable of deserting him. At the same time, it would be foolish to assert that the matter was as profoundly important to him as to them, or that he had not many alleviations to console him for his share in this internal strife. He was surrounded by variety and novelty at the very moment when his friends were feeling to the bottom of their hearts the neglect and isolation in which they found themselves. He had two lives, while they had but one. His outdoor existence, which was passed among all the wonderful historic scenes and great recollections of Rome, strengthened him for the inner one, which was so sadly overcast. One day it was Lacordaire who accompanied him to localities which, both in their Christian and pagan associations, were overflowing with interest to both. Another time Rio would be his companion—Rio, who knew and could expound everything, but who at this moment was rapt, he tells us, in an indolent and genial state of non-exertion, scarcely to be roused even by frescoes or catacombs. And, on the other side, he had Albert, with whom he could wander over the sunny slopes of Pincio, listening for hours together, with all the sympathy of his years, to the beginnings of that love-tale which all readers are now acquainted with. These varieties of life must have made the slow days more tolerable, as they lingered on one by one; and doubtless there were many hours, or even days, in which he could escape altogether from all those questions of what the Pope would do— from all those chill doubts as to final success— from the mortification of neglect, and the painful thought of going back again, disowned and discouraged, to that France which the three friends had left with such proud confidence. Albert, besides making him the confidant of his love, had even ventured to take Montalembert to the Casa Margherita, where dwelt the beautiful Countess d'Alopeus and her daughter, the gentle and beloved Alexandrine of the ' Recit d'une Sœur,' who sang soft songs to them, and charmed the very hearts out of their bosoms. Albert had no sooner done this, it is true, than he fell into visionary jealousy of his friend, whose genius and gifts were greater than his own; but young Montalembert, though he looked on with a mixture of interest and envy at his friend's romance, had not yet reached for himself that moment of supreme youthful emotion.

Thus the young man had a double life in the midst of all those treasures of art, and the associations to which even the least sensitive are more or less susceptible, in Rome. He had his Dante ever at hand, which he studied with enthusiasm, and which moved his mind to those historical researches which were always dear to him. And with his "Master" to look up to (notwithstanding that in one matter he might doubt his perfect judiciousness), and with Rio, Albert, and Lacordaire (notwithstanding their many discussions) to love him and bear him continual company, perhaps he was not, on the whole, much to be pitied. Even Lacordaire, though the matter was more important to him, seems to have found also a certain alleviation in his surroundings. "I see him still," says Montalembert, "wandering for long days among the ruins and monuments, stopping now and then as if lost in admiration, with that exquisite feeling for true beauty which never left him, gazing upon all that is unique and wonderful in Rome, moved above all by the tranquil and unequalled charm of her horizons; then returning to the common hearth to preach resignation, submission, and reason to M. de la Mennais." Thus whatever varieties might break their life and charm them into forgetfulness, every evening, every return to the common roof, brought them back to the common burden, as, after all inter-

ruptions and alleviations, the heart of man re-
turns continually to its prevailing care, whatever that may happen to be.

At length, after some weeks of this discouraging neglect, they asked an interview with the
Pope. Before this was granted, they were required to draw up a formal account of their
views and intentions, and what it was they
wanted. It was Lacordaire who was selected
to do this; and though he did it with a heart
which had begun to tremble, no doubt his plea
was both forcible and eloquent. After a long
interval their audience was granted to them.
They were presented to the Pope by the Cardinal de Rohan, representative of one of the old-
est and greatest houses of French nobility, and
an old and constant friend of Montalembert.
Never was there a better evidence of the mode
in which Rome treats her rash children than
this interview. They were very well received
—benevolently and graciously—poor pilgrims,
who had come with such a high intent! "He
treated us with the kindness natural to him,"
says Montalembert, "without the shadow of a
reproach; but he made not the slightest allu-
sion to the matter which had brought us to
Rome." "The Pope received us graciously, but
without saying a single word of our business,"

says Lacordaire. The bewildering character of
such a reception, more discouraging, more overwhelming than opposition, may readily be conceived. There was "not the shadow of a reproach;" only their enthusiasm, their zeal, their
foolish fervour were thrown back upon their own
hearts. Support, strength, hope, or consolation
were not to be found there. For this they had
rashly left their life, with all its occupations and
possibilities; for this they had travelled and
waited and hoped. Who can wonder that the
soul of a visionary like Lamennais was filled
with indignant bitterness? Some time afterwards, the secretary of Cardinal Pacca brought
a letter from his master to the disappointed
party. "It arrived very early," says Lacordaire,
"and I took it immediately to M. de la Mennais, who was not yet up. Its substance was
that the Holy Father did justice to our good
intentions, but we had treated supremely delicate questions without the moderation which
was desirable; that these questions should be
examined, but that in the mean time we might
return to our own country, where we should be
told, when the proper moment came, what the
decision was."

Here, then, was the end at once of their
enterprise and the long suspense in which they

had been held. Lamennais would not believe even the evidence of his senses. "He read Cardinal Pacca's letter coldly," says Lacordaire, "and announced to me that he would remain in Rome and await the decision promised us." Montalembert gives a still more graphic account of this interview, in the early brightness of the spring morning at the bedside of the master. When the letter had been read, he says, "Lacordaire placed resolutely before him this alternative —'Either we ought not to have come at all, or else we must now submit and be silent.' The Abbé de la Mennais refused to accept this conclusion. "I will demand an immediate decision," he said, "and will await it at Rome; after that, I will decide what to do." After this painful conflict of sentiment, Lacordaire, with his heart full, rushed into the room of his younger friend and communicated the letter to him. "I found Montalembert," he says, "disposed to follow the example of our common master." Thus the pilgrim band was torn asunder—the two elders in direct and declared opposition, the youngest of all still more torn asunder than they, agreeing with one by the reason and with the other by the heart. Lacordaire left Rome very soon after, feeling that the pledge of submission under which he had come, as well as many other serious inducements,

demanded this step of him. " After several days
of melancholy reflection," he says, " I thought I
owed it to myself to decline the responsibility of
what seemed to me a great mistake ; and on the
15th March 1832, I set out for France alone, with
the saddest presentiments, and after the most
melancholy farewells. M. de la Mennais was
not accustomed to be opposed, and disagreement
appeared to him almost treason. M. de Montalembert, whose friendship with me was still
but of short standing, was wounded by perceiving that my reason was stronger than my
affections."

Lacordaire went away sadly, feeling himself
separated from his friends, and probably not
without reason to suppose that the breach
between them was likely to be a serious one.
And the first sensation of those who were left
behind would not seem to have been painful.
Friendship has its pardonable disloyalties ; and
the departure even of a beloved critic is sometimes welcome for a season. Almost immediately
after, Rio and Albert de la Ferronays came to
occupy the place which he had left vacant ; and
no doubt his absence must to a certain extent
have been a relief, for it ended the conflict
that had been going on for weeks, and left the
younger disciple at liberty to consent to all

the master wished without a perpetual struggle against Lacordaire's arguments and the good sense which dictated them, and which found an echo in his own reasonable mind. As for Montalembert, he had evidently no wish to leave Rome, and he had the attachment of a son for Lamennais ; and when their *tête-à-tête* was broken by the arrival of the other two, who had no share in the painful burden of the past or in the anxieties of the future, an agreeable interval of quietness followed. Of this M. Rio gives us a very pleasant sketch in his Epilogue, already quoted.

" Our life was settled and regulated only from the day when we decided to join MM. de la Mennais and de Montalembert. This was a great event in the life of Albert, almost more than in my own; for my mind only derived some advantage from my subsequent relations with the Abbé de la Mennais, while Albert was to find in the friendship of M. de Montalembert, who was little older than himself, an inexhaustible sympathy with his happiness and in his suffering. We had all four a point of intellectual union in the daily reading of one or two cantos of Dante's great epic ; but neither Albert nor I were sufficiently initiated in that divine poetry, and the progress of M. de la Mennais did not answer to the high idea which we had formed of his analytical qualities, whatever subject he might apply them to. The only one among us who was capable of resolving, in a manner at all satisfactory, the political or historical problems which even in the finest cantos of the 'Inferno' or 'Purgatorio' distract so often the enjoyment of the reader, was M. de Montalembert, who, to our great edification, kept up this study by the side of that of the Holy Scripture, as if to draw from the very fountain-head the inspirations which were to give so much brilliancy to his after-career."

There is something amusing in this picture of the young student, whose industry and power of mastering any intellectual difficulty were so much greater than those of ordinary men, dragging his whole little retinue of friends with him into the heart of the great poem which he loved—though among the three fellow-students who toiled after him in those daily readings there was not one who perfectly understood the subject of their joint studies. We doubt whether Lacordaire's independent and masterful intellect could have been led away, in the midst of so many troubles, to this daily exercise, which comes so quaintly into the story. But Montalembert would seem to have been Dante-mad at this period of his life—a delightful insanity, which is apt to seize upon those who make early acquaintance with that mighty poet in his own land. Thus a certain case of mind makes itself visible in the little circle, with time enough on its hands to read Dante every day, which is very different from the sombre air of excitement and suspense which had surrounded them before Lacordaire's departure. "Our poor little trio in Rome," Montalembert wrote years afterwards to Alexandrine, ignoring the presence of Lamennais, who by that time had dropped altogether out of sight, "where our dear Albert studied with so much zeal, and wrote volumes of notes upon the history of Italy and Tuscany, holding a little *scaldino** between his legs to keep himself warm." Thus the impetuous Dante-lover made his fellow-students work, leading them on with his own penetrating historical instincts and poetic zeal.

The only annoyance which disturbed the little domestic party in this interval of quiet was locked in M. Rio's friendly bosom, and did not affect the others ; it was that Count de la Ferronays, a most submissive Catholic and faith-

* An earthenware vase containing wood-embers which is much used in Italy in cold weather in the absence of fires.

ful Royalist, trembled to see his impressionable and sensitive son thrown into the daily society of two such red-hot revolutionaries as Lamennais and Montalembert. This alarm produced continual letters, which disturbed the good Rio very much; and in the end of April, Albert was recalled by his father to Naples, where the family were living. Montalembert made up his mind to make an excursion with them into these new and beautiful coasts; and we are again obliged to M. Rio for a delightful sketch of a part of this journey, which they made alone, Albert's health forbidding him to be of the party. Their object was to visit on foot the great Abbey of Monte Cassino, the headquarters of the Benedictine order, which all travellers from Rome to Naples must recollect, seated upon its lofty height, and looking over the great plain as it spreads into the blue horizon and bluer sea. It is curious to note how early the future biographer of St Benedict and his order was moved to make this pious pilgrimage. "He took more interest in seeing this famous abbey than in all the other interesting places on our way," says Rio; unawares his life already wove itself in with the names that were to occupy so great a place in its later records. Here is a sketch of the outset of this journey in that delightful April of Italy which is more sweet than summer, the very season of poetry and youth :—

"The first day was delicious. The weather was beautiful, and the country still more so. Each of us had his Dante, and as we went we read aloud alternately, taking up the poem at the place where we had left off in our readings with the Abbé de la Mennais; that is to say, at the beginning of the 'Purgatorio,' which I then read for the first time. I can still recollect the colour of the sky, the snake which rushed across our path, the distant perspective, and the far-off sounds which struck our eyes and ears, when my companion began to read, in tones full of emotion, the first lines of the eighth canto—lines which ought never to be read except at sea or in the depth of the country, within the sound of some village bell.

> 'Era già l'ora che volge il disio
> Ai naviganti, e'interisce il cuore
> Lo dì che han detto a dolci amici addio,
>   E che lo novo peregrin d'amore
> Punge, se ode squilla di lontano
> Che paia il giorno pianger che si muore.'

"There was still light enough to read, with the slowness which my imperfect knowledge required, the two or three following cantos up to that beautiful paraphrase of the Lord's Prayer,

> ' Oh Padre nostro che ne' cieli stai,'

which seems made expressly for fatigued travellers."

This little incident reveals to us as in a picture the poetic journey—but whether they attained the heights of Monte Cassino in this lingering and interrupted way we are not informed. From Naples they went to Amalfi, where Albert, with his absorbing romance, was once more of the party; and in the company of the young lover, who was capable of little but to babble of *Her*, Montalembert spent a month of refreshing leisure. Notwithstanding the graver anxieties in his own mind, and the lively sense of ridicule which was already developed in him, he entered into all these confidences with a sympathy which gave strength and consolation to the young lover. " You were never either cold or sarcastic with me," Albert wrote immediately after they had parted company. " You understand everything; and now that you are here no longer, I have such need of you ! " Only a very large and many-sided mind could have answered to all the claims at present made upon him. Between Lamennais, in his anger and disappointment, obstinately lingering in Rome, and inaccessible to reason so far as one question was concerned, and Albert, indifferent to everything in the world but *Elle*, what a difference there was! but both had his ear, his attention, and his sympathy, full and lavish, bestowed without restriction or *arrière pensée*. He counselled Albert how to manage the delicate affairs in which *Elle* was concerned with as much gravity and good faith as though a kingdom had been in question; and he returned out of the travels and pursuits which he loved, to support and succour the master, who fumed and fretted at Rome without a word of complaint, though it is doubtful whether his convictions ever went entirely with those of Lamennais; and it is certain that this state of semi-rebellion against the decision of the Church was always painful and distressing to him. From the middle of May to the middle of July, two of those blazing summer months in which Rome is like a furnace, and every soul that can quit her burning streets flies to the refuge of the woods or the hills, Montalembert remained with Lamennais, doing all he could to calm and subdue him. This martyrdom was of a very silent sort, unrewarded and unapplauded, but it is the hardest kind of self-sacrifice.

By the middle of July, however, even Lamennais seems to have given up the hope of any reply from the Pope to his urgent applications;

and at last he allowed himself to be persuaded
to leave Rome, and to join in an art-pilgrimage
into Germany, under the guidance of Rio, upon
which Montalembert had set his heart. Before
he left Rome, however, he announced his intention of resuming the 'Avenir' on his return
to Paris, accepting the silence of the Holy See
as a consent to his so doing. Thus his last
step was to provoke the thunders which had so
long slumbered. With this final flourish of
trumpets the pilgrims departed, in a mood of
mind very different from that with which they
had arrived in Italy. They went to Munich,
where they remained for some weeks, and where
Lamennais, after the long hush of enforced silence
which had occurred in his life, plunged with eager
relish into the argumentations of the religious
and Catholic school of German theologians then
reigning in Munich, and of which M. Rio was
an impassioned disciple. We are not told what
share or interest Montalembert took in these
discussions. Probably it was not great, for the
bent of his mind was not towards theological
discussion; but no doubt to Lammenais the
sense that he was on familiar ground, and once
more able to maintain his own part fearlessly
against equal opponents, must have had a soft-
ening and ameliorating influence, predisposing

him towards the more submissive attitude
which he afterwards assumed. And Munich,
then in all the early enthusiasm of reviving art,
with its new school of Christian painters working in the full sunshine of royal favour, must
have afforded a crowd of new interests to Montalembert. Very soon, too, a pleasure of a different kind, a joyous surprise, came upon him.
Lacordaire, who had passed these later months
sadly and obscurely in Paris, bearing the burden
of his rashness even after he had withdrawn from
it, on hearing of Lamennais's expressed determination to resume the 'Avenir,' went off secretly
into Germany, in order to avoid all occasion of
fruitless meetings and discussions, and to detach himself completely from all possibility of
being drawn into a new and rebellious undertaking. " In order to escape from the necessity
of breaking publicly with my companions in
arms, or following them against my will in the
ruin which they were preparing for themselves,
I rushed," he says, " into Germany, with the intention of hiding myself there for some months.
I chose Munich for no other reason than that I
had heard living was cheap there." He arrived
in ignorance that the very persons whom he
wished to avoid were established in the same town
before him ; but the melancholy young priest

had scarcely found a lodging and settled himself in his spare little chamber, where he meant to live cheaply and keep himself hidden from the world, when the door opened, and Montalembert suddenly appeared. He had found out his friend's arrival by the list of strangers published in the papers, and with his usual impetuosity lost not an hour in seeking him out. No doubt their reunion, notwithstanding all the painful circumstances involved, was to both a great happiness, for the dissension between them was very slight and easily healed. And it is very probable that Montalembert's joy in renewing his intercourse with Lacordaire was increased by the hope of finding in him a pleader more effectual than himself to deter their master from further resistance.

Throughout all this time of agitation, indeed, Montalembert's position is very attractive and engaging. He stands to Lamennais in the relationship which we sometimes see a sensible son or daughter in common life occupy towards an impetuous parent. The young observer, free of the passions which move the elder, sees all his rashness, the unfortunate steps he takes, the unhappy words he speaks in heat and irritation, with a heart half broken by distress and powerlessness to help; yet clings to the hasty father with double loyalty, defending him hotly out of doors, while timidly, tearfully remonstrating within. And what delight it is to a young soul, so torn asunder between love and disapproval, to see some powerful advocate of the wiser way come in, whom he backs up with glances of encouragement, with whispered prayers, which in his heart he feels as half a crime! This was Montalembert's position. He was too young, too inexperienced, to express boldly all the vague trouble and disapprobation that was in his own mind; but when, to his delight and wonder, he found the name of Lacordaire in the Munich paper, like an angel sent from heaven to his aid, it was with double eagerness that he rushed to him, longing to see him for love's sake, and longing still more for his influence and help. No doubt it required some trouble and many entreaties to induce Lacordaire thus to rush into the very meeting he had fled out of Paris to avoid. But his flight itself had been prompted by a desire to keep from an open breach, and this no doubt aided the importunities of his friend. Finally, they went together to Lamennais's room. "He received me with visible displeasure," says Lacordaire, "but the meeting was a solemn one. We entered into conversation, and for two hours I exerted myself to show him how vain was his hope of resuming the 'Avenir,' and how such a step would be against at once reason, good faith, and honour. At last, whether it was that my arguments had convinced him, or that my separation from the undertaking made some impression upon him, he said to me these words, ' Yes, you are right; your conclusion is just.'" The reader will easily imagine the comfort given by this reply to the eager soul of Montalembert, who sat looking from one to another with an anxiety he could not conceal, putting in now and then his modest word, supporting the wise counsel with all the secret force of his sympathy and prayers, though never for a moment swerving from the loyal devotion which bound him to support his master, even where he could not altogether agree or sympathise.

The momentary victory thus obtained was very soon put to the proof. Next day the philosophers, authors, and artists of Munich, among whom the French visitors had been living—uniting, as it seems so much easier for men of their professions to unite anywhere than in England—gave a dinner outside the walls of Munich to the distinguished strangers. It was Lamennais who was the special guest, but his younger friends were glorified by the surrounding of his fame. When the feast was nearly over, Lamennais was called out from the table; and it was at this moment of friendly ease and enjoyment that the Encyclical letter of Gregory XVI., which condemned at once his principles and his enterprise, was placed in his hand. He ran his eyes over it hastily; and very likely in that genial atmosphere, after all the laudations of which no doubt he had been the object, its condemnation fell more lightly upon him than it would have done had he read it in his chamber. His friends watched him with anxiety, seeing that something important had come, and impatient and uneasy to know what it was. Lacordaire's arguments, the pleasure of reunion with him, the hearty applause and worship of the German sympathisers round him, — all must have moved Lamennais to a favourable interpretation of what he read. The party went out after their meal to a neighbouring village for coffee, and on the way Lamennais told what had happened in an undertone to the two colleagues, who rushed to his side as they went out to hear the news. " I have received an encyclical of the Pope against us. We must not hesitate to submit," he said. Thus he took

the step they had so prayed and hoped he
would, and so feared he would not take, with
all the ease of a foregone conclusion. It was so
much better than they hoped, that the young
men followed him with tremulous excitement
and anxiety, after the interrupted entertain-
ment of the evening, to his rooms, where at
once "he made out in a few lines, short but
precise, an act of obedience, with which the
Pope was satisfied."

"God," says Lacordaire, piously, "had thus
brought us together at Munich to sign a joint
and sincere adhesion to the will of the Father
of the faithful, without distinction, without restriction." The younger disciples were at the
height of joy; all their old love 'and admiration for their leader was doubled. They carried him off, as it were, in triumph to France,
"vanquished victors," as Lacordaire says with
enthusiasm, conscious of having done their best,
and conscious of having crowned that best with
the highest self-renunciation—the sacrifice of
their own will to that of their spiritual head.
It was with a certain swell of triumph that they
made this journey, more happy almost than if
they had been successful, in that strange passion of half-weeping joy, with which children
applaud the father who has turned aside in

time from an error they thought him certain to fall into. "The sacrifice of M. de la Mennais was much greater than ours," says even the moderate Lacordaire, who was never a worshipper of the master; "we were young, he was fifty; he was the chief, we were only private soldiers." Thus they took him back on their shoulders, on their hearts, blowing a hundred trumpets. It was a downfall indeed; but the downfall was as glorious as any victory.

It is unnecessary for us to follow further the history of Lamennais and Lacordaire. They went together to Brittany, but soon separated, being two souls of utterly different constitution, which only could have come together under some arbitrary impulsion. And when Lamennais had regained his solitude of La Chesnaie, and read at his leisure that Encyclical which he had accepted so hastily, other sentiments less submissive arose in his mind—sentiments which, setting his priesthood apart, and the submission which was his duty as a Catholic, were natural enough in the breast of a sincere and honest man, whose opinions were genuine. In this Encyclical letter, which is dated the 15th August 1832, Pope Gregory declared that it is "from the infected fountain of indifferentism that the absurd and erroneous maxim—or rather the delusion—

that liberty of conscience must be assured and guaranteed, has flowed. The way to this pernicious error is prepared by that liberty of opinion without limit, which is spreading far and near to the danger of society, both religious and secular, and of which certain impudent persons have affirmed that there may arise an advantage to religion." The Encyclical goes on to forbid all resistance against authority, of whatsoever kind. "Let all consider that, according to the saying of the apostle, all power comes from God. Thus he who resists power resists the ordinance of God. Both divine and human laws rise up against those who attempt, by the shameful plots of revolt and sedition, to shake the fidelity of the people to their princes, and to cast them down from the throne. The first Christians, in the midst of the fury of persecution, served the emperors faithfully. These fine examples of inviolable submission to princes—a submission which is the necessary consequence of the precepts of the Christian religion—condemn the detestable insolence and wickedness of those who, inflamed by the heat of an audacious liberty, use all their efforts to shake and overthrow the rights of kings." The liberty of the press is entitled "a fatal liberty, which cannot be too much hated and cursed." This was the

document which had procured instant submission and abandonment of all their projects from
the three pilgrims united at Munich ; and we
repeat it is little wonderful that, when the leader
of that religious crusade which had taken " God
and liberty " for its device — read over carefully and slowly the sentence thus pronounced
against him, a change came over those meek dis-
positions of submission which had so overjoyed
his younger friends.   Lamennais has little more
to do with our immediate narrative ; but the
question of this submission is so interesting and
important in the late as well as in the early life
of Montalembert, that we cannot but pause to
consider the matter more fully than can be done
in the midst of a narrative : this, however, we
prefer to do in a separate chapter, which the
reader, who may be indifferent on the subject,
may pass over if it pleases him—and in the
mean time conclude this part of our story.

Montalembert remained in Paris, when his
friends, the vanquished victors, *vaincus vic-
torieux*, retired to the country.   He established himself in a little apartment in the
old aristocratic quarter, which he never forsook, the Faubourg St Germain ; and no doubt,
with all the more enjoyment for the trial
through which he had just passed, entered

again into those modest and refined pleasures of society which a man can enjoy who has
it in his power to call around him the highest spirits of his time. He was now nearly
three-and-twenty, still a youth, but ripened into
manhood by conflict and trial, and by the re-
sponsibilities of a public position which he had
taken upon him so early. He was very lonely,
sadly debarred from those domestic enjoyments
which were already dear to him, left by himself
in that great wilderness of Paris to make out life
as he could. His mother had settled in England,
his young brother was a student at the Military
School, and he had no near relations to stand in
the place of his own family to him. We shall
see further on how deeply he felt all this; but
in the mean time we may quote an account of
his manner of life, in one particular at least, as
given by Frederic Ozanam, a man of congenial
mind, whose pursuits and desires were all like
his own. It is dated in January 1833, a few
months after the events above described.

"M. de Montalembert receives his friends
every Sunday evening; there is a great deal of
varied and expansive talk; punch and cakes
are served to the visitors, who come and go in
bands, four or five friends together. I reckon

upon going now and then. Last Sunday I saw
there MM. de Coux, D'Ault-Dumesnil, Mickiewicz, a great Lithuanian poet, Werner de Merode,
whose father the Belgians think of electing their
king, and Sainte-Beuve. An odour of brotherhood and of Catholicism breathes through these
little parties. M. de Montalembert has an angelic countenance, and is very brilliant in conversation. He is a good story-teller, and extremely well informed.

"The points of doctrine on which Rome has
required silence are never brought in question.
In this respect the wisest discretion is kept up;
but literature, history, the interests of the poor,
the progress of civilisation, are largely discussed.
The conversation is animated, the speakers
grow excited sometimes, our hearts are warmed
—and one carries away a feeling of satisfaction
and pure pleasure, good resolutions and courage
for the future."

Curious glimpse into a life which had changed
itself, thrown aside its favourite occupations, put
a seal upon its lips in obedience to the mandate
of the Pope ; and all this at twenty-three, and
in the nineteenth century ! To us, in our different existence, regulated by laws and customs
so diverse, the idea is almost too astounding to

be credible. We refrain for the moment from endeavouring to explain it. But when the reader considers what manner of young man this was, how full of fire and enthusiasm, how brilliantly endowed by nature, how overflowing with activity, he will be unable to pass it over with the ordinary smile of wondering contempt at the mixture of superstition in his character which made such a sacrifice possible. Such a man could not but have had some way of accounting to himself for such a strange submission, and he could not but have had a strong motive, whether comprehensible or not to us.

During this year Montalembert made several journeys through France, and at least one into Belgium. These expeditions, however, whether taken up specially in the interests of Art or not, revealed to the young observer, whose eyes were so keen and clear, and whom nothing escaped, the neglected condition of the great architectural monuments of France, the noble old buildings, both ecclesiastical and secular, of the middle ages. His love of everything that was beautiful, his inclination towards the picturesque history of the Ages of Faith, and, above all, his fervent Catholic spirit, made this question profoundly interesting to him ; and in the very beginning of the year 1833 he assailed the world on the subject in an eloquent and energetic article, entitled "Du Vandalisme en France," which was published in March, in the 'Revue des deux Mondes.' In this long and able paper his style showed itself fully formed, pruned down out of the luxuriance of the 'Avenir,' but still retaining much of the rush and ardour, the sweeping torrent of life, which were so evident in the lyrical outbursts of his early youth, and which continued to his latest day to animate every subject he touched. Like every young patriotic critic, the indignant writer took it for granted that his own country enjoyed an unhappy pre-eminence in this national crime.

"It is only in France that Vandalism reigns alone and without restraint," he cries. "The ancient soil of our country, surcharged as it was with the most marvellous creations of the imagination and faith, becomes day by day more naked, more uniform, more bare— nothing is spared. The devastating axe attacks alike forests and churches, castles and hotels de ville. One would say that the intention of our contemporaries was to persuade themselves that the world began yesterday, and was to end to-morrow, so anxious are they to annihilate everything whose duration exceeds the life of a man. Even the ruins which we create ourselves are not respected; and while we hear that in England the great proprietors spend every year a considerable income in preserving those which are on their lands, and that in Germany the people hold their Liberal meetings within the ruins of their old castles, as if to put their new-born liberties under the protection of the past, among ourselves we do not even leave Time to do his natural work; we refuse to Nature her motherly mourning. For Nature, always gentle and loving, is specially so in respect to the ruins which man has made : she seems to take pleasure in ornamenting them with her most beautiful decorations, as if to console them for their nakedness and desolation. But we tear away their shroud of verdure, their crowns of flowers; we violate the graves of past ages. The ancient noble puts them up to auction, the new citizen buys them; and if he does not condescend to give them a place in his new constructions, he patches them up and embellishes them according to his fancy. Both unite in order to dishonour those relics of the past."

The critic goes on to enumerate the enemies of art, and to classify the different kinds of

Vandals, who placed every old building in the country in danger.

"Modern Vandalism divides itself into two classes, very different in their motives, but bringing about a similar result. These two modes of operation may be distinguished by the name of destructive and reconstructive Vandalism. Each of these ideas is carried out by very different classes of Vandals, whom I range in the following order, assigning to each the rank which its violence against everything that is antique (*contre les vieilleries*) merits :—

I.—DESTRUCTIVE VANDALISM.

First Class. The Government.
Second „   Maires and Municipal Councils.
Third   „   Proprietors.
Fourth „   Conseils de Fabriques and the Clergy.

"In the fifth place, and at a long distance from the above, Insurrection.

II.—RECONSTRUCTIVE VANDALISM.

First Class. The Clergy and Conseils de Fabriques.
Second „   The Government.
Third   „   Municipal Councils.
Fourth „   Proprietors.

"Insurrections have at least the advantage of restoring nothing."

This article was written in the form of a letter to Victor Hugo, the head of the Romantic school in literature, and the very earliest beginner of that crusade in favour of religious art which has been more successful than Montalembert's campaign for religious liberty. "It is impossible," says the young writer, addressing the already celebrated poet, "for any one to occupy himself with our national art, our historical monuments, the sublime relics of our past, without at once thinking of you, who, the the first in France, have constituted yourself the champion of that cause." Two years before, Montalembert had reviewed 'Nôtre Dame de Paris' in the 'Avenir,' dwelling with enthusiasm upon all the splendid framework of that wonderful tale, while gently and modestly rebuking the less commendable details of the extraordinary romance woven in with it; but even these imperfections did not lessen his enthusiasm for the great genius, which since then has wasted itself in so many strange vagaries.

His only other literary work of this year was a preface to a book of Polish poetry, the 'Livre des Pelerins Polonais,' by Adam Mickiewicz, fragments of which are still included in his collected works. The reason of its mutilated condition is, that this little production fell also under the censure of Rome, for Lamennais had filled the atmosphere with commotion, and stray discharges of Papal artillery continued for some time to disturb all the echoes. The preface was condemned in a letter written by the Pope to the Bishop of Rennes; and it would almost seem as if Lamennais had a certain malicious pleasure in seeing his disciple touched by the censure which had fallen so heavily on himself. "Puisque le vin est tiré, il faut le boire," he wrote; and notwithstanding Montalembert's remonstrances against the work upon which he was himself engaged—'Les Paroles d'un Croyant'—he proceeded to complete it, and to justify the condemnation. Grieved by this new venture, alarmed by all the results it might produce, and sick of those imbittering and endless controversies, Montalembert made up his mind to withdraw for a time from France and from the society of his master. It was not that he loved the master less, or was less anxious to serve and succour him. He had indeed for some time made a regular yearly contribution to his support, which he kept up anxiously through all their divisions, and would gladly have done anything to withdraw him from the fatal circle of irritation, rebellion, and doubt which began to close around him.

But he could not waste his own life in futile attempts to save Lamennais; and he had still some objects in life, some favourite studies, and at least one friend who could share his labours. Politics were interdicted to him, but history and art were free. Accordingly, he resolved to return to Germany. As early as May, immediately after the publication of his article " Du Vandalisme," he had written to Rio, then in England, the following invitation and appeal :—

" My friend, I feel more than ever that it is impossible for me to travel—that is, to rush about the world for the purposes of curiosity, without you. The only person who could replace you would be Albert; but I don't know what he is doing with himself. In heaven's name, leave thy England, and come here a little that we may arrange matters. You have been for six months in that country of fogs. Come and make yourself a little like a Frenchman again."

Rio was not deaf to this appeal. He would seem to have joined Montalembert at the little town of Ploërmel, in Brittany, from whence they went together to see Lamennais, or were joined by him there; and some brief moment of loving intercourse was between the three, who seem then to have met all together for the last time. La Chesnaie had already witnessed one separation — the sad departure of Lacordaire; and even this meeting was overcast by the bitter complaints and sarcasms of Lamennais against Rome and its decisions — complaints which, however he may have been tempted temporarily to share them, never seem to have found any real echo in Montalembert's heart. This may be said to have been his final severance from the master of his youthful enthusiasm. Both were changing day by day, dropping further apart from each other. They parted with mutual affection, and continued a most close and tender correspondence for some time; and they had at least one more personal interview after Montalembert's return. But the golden chain was broken, and never to be permanently reunited. Montalembert left Paris that autumn, and made his way into Germany, with many painful and distracted thoughts, but once more an object, such as it was,—and found a new and congenial work awaiting him, and the beginning of a happier life.

CHAPTER VII.

CATHOLIC SUBMISSION.

THE transaction which we have just recorded is one of the most curious in recent history. In the fulness of the nineteenth century, in the very atmosphere of revolution, two young men, ingenuous and proud, true children of their generation, full of liberal ideas and opinions, loving freedom, and jealous of any attempt to curb the progress of free institutions, suddenly stopped short in their career, gave up their most cherished projects, relinquished an occupation they loved, and if they did not adopt, at least consented to the proclamation of doctrines which they hated, keeping silence upon their own. This sudden change is as wonderful as ever revolution was, and its motives are more mysterious than those which have determined any revolution. Had they anything to gain by it? No; on the contrary, their lives were torn from their habitual places, and all was for a time chaos around them. Were they fools or bigots incapable of judging what they were about to do? No; on the contrary, one of them at least was the very impersonation at once of genius and good sense; and in the other enthusiasm was already tempered by a keenness of mental vision sometimes almost harsh in its vivacity. What, then, was the cause? They were men of good judgment and vigorous imagination both—neither of them likely to escape from those obstinate questionings of the mind with which every man is more or less assailed when he has taken a decided step in any new direction, or changed his course of action. Had they done it unadvisedly, on some hasty impulse which seemed to promise harmony and reunion, it would have been less remarkable. But they do not seem to have had any thought of this. They did it simply because it appeared to them their duty; their best way of serving God, their most honourable course towards men. The question is so strange, so intricate, so all but incomprehensible to us, that it demands the most patient consideration. Of course it is much easier to point to it as an instance of the great defect of the Roman Catholic system, and the astonishing superstition or servility of the

Catholic mind, than to make any endeavour to enter into its real causes. In all controverted questions it is always the easiest way to conclude that your opponent is deluded, or guilty, or a fool; and there is no opinion more generally held on this side of the Channel than that the life of such a man as Montalembert is a mistake, wilfully stultified by his own action, and made useless to humanity in secular matters because of its subserviency in matters spiritual. This, however, is not only an uncomfortable doctrine, and one which may be equally applied to ourselves by any obtuse intelligence which declines to make any attempt to understand us; but it is at the same time wholly uninstructive, throwing no light to us upon human nature; but, on the contrary, closing the door between us and some of our fellow-creatures, whom it might be very well worth our while to understand. And it is certain that no man can be understood when he is looked at, not from his own point of view, but from the spectator's, whose views and beliefs and training have been totally different from his. It is hard to start with, for us, to whom the liberty of private judgment is the very foundation of all intellectual and spiritual life, to understand a man who carefully and rigorously limits that liberty, and in one class of subjects relinquishes it altogether; therefore caution and care are all the more necessary when we attempt to decide upon the character of that man's motives and the spring of his actions.

And in the first place, we must premise that Lacordaire and Montalembert both belonged to that class which is to be found in all countries and varieties of faith, and which by temperament and conviction is more devoted to the Church than to the State. With such men, religious influences hold a place higher than any other; and though there have been many instances in which they have combined with this sentiment great devotion to the State also, yet the former has always been more momentous, more all-important to them. The class is perhaps pretty fairly divided in political opinions, yet leaning most to Conservatism by a curious natural process which acts upon both sides. The earnest Churchman is moved towards Conservatism by the fact that a quiet maintenance of the *statu quo*, whatever that may be, in politics, is best for the work of religion; he believes that political excitement distracts men's minds from matters much more important, and consequently he is disposed, in perhaps a majority of cases, to lend his support to the powers that be. The political man, on

the other hand, however liberal in his opinions,
who does not like to be troubled by the heat
and commotion produced by religious struggles, is constantly found to be conservative in
Church matters for the very same reason. By
nature, more than by training, Charles de Montalembert belonged to this class, of whom it
used to be said in Scotland, that they would do
everything for the State, and a good deal more
for the Church. Lacordaire belonged to it, not
by training nor perhaps by nature, but by conviction. To both of them the one thing need-
ful, the absolutely indispensable influence for
men, was that of Religion. Fervent in their
love of free institutions, and in their hatred of
tyranny, they were yet influenced beyond all
other motives by an anxious wish to convert, to
purify, to save the souls and amend the lives of
their countrymen. To secure them against the
tyranny of secular government; yes—to watch
jealously over the Charter, the Constitution,
permitting no infringement of the rights which
it guaranteed,—these were objects dear to their
hearts, and which roused them to enthusiasm;
but that which filled them with still deeper
enthusiasm was the idea of a nation converted
to God, endowed with the divine Charter of
salvation, and holding its faith and the observ-

ances of religion dearer than any other rights. To his life's end there never was a movement for constitutional and popular freedom which did not secure the instant interest of Montalembert, which did not swell his voice and light up his eyes with sympathy; but above all this, and still more precious, he held the progress of religion, not refusing an honest and warm admiration to the piety even which he considered to be built upon a wrong foundation. His readers and friends are alike aware with what thorough appreciation and regretful tenderness he spoke and wrote of the religious spirit of England, contrasting it, almost with tears, with the condition of orthodox France. He had that rare candour of soul which permits a man to perceive the qualities he loves even in his opponent. Thus almost in any form religion was dear to him—dearer than everything else; and the spread of what he believed to be true religion was his highest and most cherished mission in this world.

Having made this proviso to begin with, let us recall Montalembert's account of the effect which Rome at the first glance produced upon Lacordaire. It was the young priest's first visit to that centre of the faith he adored, and the impression which it made upon him was great. Perhaps there is no place in the world which affects strangers with sentiments so profound and so different. On Lamennais, for instance, who had been there before, and whose soul was weary with the contradictions of life, its influence was altogether evil. "One of the most joyful days of my life," he cries, "will be that on which I shall leave this great sepulchre, where nothing is to be found but bones and worms;" and he goes on to congratulate himself that his life is not destined to be spent in that "moral desert," where faith and love are sought for vainly "in the midst of old ruins, upon which the vilest human passions sun themselves like unclean reptiles." Lacordaire was moved in a totally different way. The view of the old metropolis of Christianity silenced and solemnised his mind. In the words which we have already quoted, "He, a journalist and citizen of 1830, a Liberal and Democrat, understood at the first glance not only the inviolable majesty of the supreme pontificate, but its difficulties, its long and patient plans, and the expedients indispensable to the government of men on this earth." The miseries and infirmities inseparable from every economy in which the human is mixed up with the divine did not escape him, but they appeared to him drowned in the mysterious splendour of tradition and authority. In short, Rome revealed itself to Lacordaire as a sort of visible incarnation of the Church and the principle of religion—an ever-living eternal principle, to which the systems of this world are but as the insects that live and die in a day. He saw, or thought he saw, how insignificant, in the presence of this everlasting reality, were all the vicissitudes of politics and the developments of civilisation ; and at the same time he perceived all the strength which was given to every religious worker by the very existence of this great Power, making but secondary account of secular matters, and watching over the great organisation of the Church in a way to secure its interest and progress through all, whether thrones stood or fell, whether nations rose or declined, faithful to the one great idea of Catholic Christianity. This conception took hold upon the young man's ardent mind with all the force of a revelation. He realised, with a sudden thrill of soul and being, the greatness, the consistency, the antiquity of Rome; how it had lived and watched, and had patience, subordinating everything to its great purpose, taking advantage of everything which could aid that purpose, yet never acknowledging anything in the world as of equal importance with its own holy and sacred cause.

There are many people who consider that cause to be the cause of spiritual tyranny, the subjection of the world to the greatest and most penetrating of despotisms—a power which controls and overrides the intellect, which contradicts and despises reason, and which lays upon men's shoulders burdens too terrible to be borne. But this was not Lacordaire's opinion. To him it was religion pure and undefiled, which was the cause of Rome. To his thinking, it was the best of all influences that went out from her in pure and fertilising streams to enrich and purify all the nations. For hundreds of years had not she poured out blessings upon the world? and it was her vocation now, her paramount mission, to watch that all was going well with religion, to think of that chiefly, to consider its interests, and not what was abstractly good or best in secular affairs.

This steady, long, persistent purpose seized hold of his imagination — he was overawed by it. After all, what were his own hot and sudden theories of a day, that he should come to vex with them the ear of this great mother, which was intent to hear over all the world the marching of her sacred armies, and the blessed footsteps of those who carry over mountain and desert the glad tidings of peace?

He felt himself like a fretful child thrusting its frivolous pains and troubles upon the mother who is a queen, and whose mind is occupied with the affairs of a great kingdom. To such a child it is enough if the royal mother turns to him for a moment, lays her soothing hand upon his head, and passes on, without time to consider his plaints, to her own more majestic business. He was half ashamed, half grieved, to have made his petty appeal, vexing her in the midst of all her lofty cares. Before she had said a word in reply, he had shrunk back, feeling his prayer out of place and untimely. To convert the world, to save souls, to promote holiness and obedience and the love of God, these were the real matters which filled her mind. Even an earthly mother more nobly occupied could not be expected to pronounce if this toy was good or not, if this game was or was not to be pursued. And what were all these varying affairs of the world, the poor illusions of political life, the excitements of the moment, but toys and games in comparison with that vast and wise supervision of interests so much greater, to which day and night, through all vicissitudes of time, through revolution and quiet, through peace and war, she gave her high attention? Some such lofty ideal conception as this seized upon the mind of Lacordaire. When we consider that it was he who suggested the pilgrimage, it is easy to conceive what his rapid conviction of its inappropriateness must have cost him. He was startled, touched, awed by his discovery. A mother in such circumstances may not always be guarded in her expressions, may send the importunate child away hurriedly, or even harshly, in her preoccupation; but that preoccupation is more than an excuse, it is a sublime and overwhelming answer to all possibilities of objection.

This was how it was that Lacordaire submitted instantly, submitted before his submission was called for, feeling instinctively that his appeal was mistaken, and, in the true sense of the word, impertinent. This was the soul and sentiment of his conduct; and it had, besides, a practical side, which, in face of present events, especially calls for our attention. As his imagination was inspired by the consistency, the unity, the patience and duration of spiritual government in Rome, so was his practical sense moved by the force of that wonderful organisation, which backs up every poor priest with the power as of a great kingdom behind him, and gives him a steadfast and powerful authority to lean upon whatever may be his own weakness.

Dissent has never thriven—nay, it has never been possible — in Roman Catholic countries. Except at the Reformation, when the great overflow of spiritual rebellion was favoured by such a combination of circumstances as has never occurred since, no man or group of men have succeeded in rebelling against Rome, and yet continued to keep up a religious character and influence. No man has been able to do it, whatever the excellence of his beginning might be, or the purity of the motives with which he started. Even in the Church of England the case of a man who separates himself from her communion is generally a painful one. He makes a commotion and excitement in the world for a time before he has fully made up his mind; and at the moment of his withdrawal he is sure of remark and notice, at all events, from certain classes. But after that brief moment he sinks flat as the spirits do in the 'Inferno,' and the dark wave pours over him, and he is heard of no more. All that sustained and strengthened and gave him a fictitious importance as the member of a great corporation has fallen away from him. He has dropped like a stone into the water—like a foundered ship into the sea. In England, however, after all has been done, there is a sea of dissent to drop into, and though his new surroundings may please him little, yet he will come out of the giddiness of his downfall to take some comfort in them—will accustom himself by degrees to the lower social level, the different spiritual atmosphere. But he who dissents from the Church of Rome has no such refuge. The moment he steps outside her fold he finds himself in outer darkness, through which awful salutations are shrieked to him by the enemies of religion, by those whom he has avoided and condemned all his life, and with whom he can agree only on the one sole article of rebellion. If he ventures to hold up his head at all after what all his friends will call his apostasy, the best that he can hope for is to be courted by heretics, professed enemies of the Church which he has been born in, and which probably he loves most dearly still, notwithstanding his disobedience. To quarrel with your home is one thing—to find its domestic laws hard, and its prejudices insupportable; but to plunge into the midst of the enemies of that home, and to hear it assailed with the virulence of ignorance —to join in gibes against your mother, and mockery of her life and motives—is a totally different matter. Yet this is almost all that a contumacious priest has to look forward to. A recent and striking example, to which we need not refer more plainly, will occur to every one who has watched the contemporary history of the Roman Catholic Church. In this case a brilliant and remarkable preacher—a man supposed the other day to be one of the most eminent and promising sons of Rome—after wavering and falling away in some points from ecclesiastical obedience, suddenly appeared in an admiring circle of gentle Anglicanism, surrounded by a fair crowd of worshipping Protestants, ready to extend to him all that broad and universal sympathy which he had no doubt been trained to regard as vilest latitudinarianism, or the readiness of Pilate to make friends with Herod. This prospect must chill the very soul of a man who has received the true priestly training, and who has been educated in that love of his Church which is of itself a noble and generous sentiment. The best thing that can happen to him is to fall among heretics ; the other alternative, and the only one, so far as events have yet made it apparent, to fall among infidels : and as his education has taught him to make but small distinction between them, and the infidels are nearer at hand, and his own countrymen, what wonder if it is into their hands that the miserable man, torn from all his ancient foundations, ejected from his natural place, heart-weary with the madness which is wrought by anger against those we love, should fall—what wonder if he should rush to the furthest extremity, hiding what he feels to be his shame, and endeavouring to take some dismal comfort in utter negation of that past from which he has been torn? Whether there are new developments in the future for the new Protesters whom a recent decision has raised up, we cannot tell. But such has been the case in the past. Life is over for the rebellious priest who breaks with his Church; his possibility of service in his vocation has come to an end; even the most careless peasant in his parish will turn from him. He is a deserter from his regiment in the face of the enemy, false to his colours, a man no longer of any human use.

And this idea no doubt glanced through the mind of Lacordaire, filling it with shuddering dread. Out of Rome there is no salvation— and, a consideration more immediate, and perhaps more telling still, out of Rome there was no Use. He trembled when he saw the edge of the precipice upon which he was standing. To set up his puny will in opposition to that of the Church—to hold by his own way and leave the way she had traced out, along which alone, walking humbly, he could serve God and man —this thought appalled him, and stopped him short in mid career.

And further still. A true Catholic is bound to receive, in matters of faith, the judgment of Rome, but not in secular matters. The encyclical letter which implied a stern condemnation of the doctrines and efforts of the 'Avenir,' consequently required the silence of its editors, and made the continuance of their paper an impossibility; but did not by any means involve their adoption of any political principles therein set forth. Once more we are compelled to avail ourselves of the simile continually employed by Roman Catholic writers. The Church, in this particular transaction, is like a mother commanding her children to abstain from something she disapproves of, and in respect to which she has a certain right to their obedience. It may happen that she is not perfectly wise in her allocution on the matter. She may mix in irrelevant subjects, she may interpolate abuse of persons in no way involved. Such things do happen sometimes in maternal, or, for that matter, paternal, commands and prohibitions; but the son who loves his mother, and who allows her right to exercise some control over him, will

accept the prohibition without by any means
necessarily accepting the general views of things
which accompany it, or the irrelevant matter
with which it is surrounded. In the very same
way Lacordaire accepted the Pope's prohibition.
He obeyed; he made the sacrifice of his own
wishes, the occupation he loved, and the immediate advocacy of a cause which he thought
worthy and noble. He was content to allow
that in everything that concerned the Church's
welfare and progress (which was what he had
intended to fight for throughout), the Church
herself, who had thought of nothing else for
eighteen hundred years, was a better judge
than he, a young man of eight-and-twenty. To
this he submitted without a question; but he
did not change his views on the other subjects
which Rome chose to interpolate. No assent,
no subscription of these doctrines was demanded
of him. He submitted to the practical necessity;
but he did not go out of his way to explain
how far he demurred or objected to the theoretical statements. They left his mind and
opinions unchanged. Even at the present day,
after the proceedings by which the late Council
have laid another bond upon Catholic souls, the
impossible burden of obedience in points of
secular opinion has never been imposed, nor can

it be so—although, no doubt, an immense pre-possession in favour of, or in opposition to, a particular theory, can always be given to a mass of people by the expressed opinion of an infallible Pope.

We have done our best to show how a man could thus pause in his career, relinquish his work, and change, as it were, the whole direction of his life and thoughts at the Papal bidding, without forfeiting his title to our respect, or really laying himself open to the reproach of servility or hypocrisy. We have done so, arguing from what we may call simple and reasonable human motives, without taking into consideration that supreme veneration for the head of his Church which every true Catholic is bound to feel. We think we have said enough to show that such a sacrifice, astounding as it was, might be still comprehensible, and need not involve any paltering with truth, or failure in personal constancy to personal conviction. It was not that these men loved political faith and loyalty less, but that they loved what they believed to be spiritual truth and obedience more.

In all this we have spoken of Lacordaire as the chief agent, though almost everything we have said refers to his younger friend and companion as well. Montalembert was very young. He was enchained, by the enthusiasm of youthful love and sympathy, to the very different nature of Lamennais; and though, we believe, always agreeing with Lacordaire in his heart, yet scarcely for the moment in a position to form an independent judgment. We take Lacordaire as the type and representative of a good Catholic, of brilliant intelligence yet perfect docility, with all the more satisfaction, however, that his was the hand which moulded the young mind of Montalembert at this particular and most trying moment, and that the same principles which we have attempted to set forth soon became part of the very nature of the younger man, and influenced his entire life.

"Les points de doctrine sur lesquels Rome a demandé le silence ne sont point remis sur le tapis. La plus sage discretion regne à cet egard," says Ozanam, in the words quoted in a previous chapter. To us this " discretion " may appear painful or pitiful according to our point of view ; but to Montalembert it was a sacrifice demanded by the highest authority known to him—a sacrifice painful but yet honourable. The hearts of the friends were sore with the necessity thus laid upon them; but they submitted with a sense that submission was their duty. The idea that it involved disgraceful weakness or unmanly servility never, we believe, once entered into their minds.

CHAPTER VIII.

THE WANDER-YEAR.—ST ELIZABETH.

WHEN Montalembert left Paris at this dreary moment, things were going very badly with him. He had lost his first object in life, and he was as yet too young to enter upon his Parliamentary career. A peer of France was not allowed to join in the public deliberations of the august body to which he belonged until he had attained the age of twenty-five, and our young traveller wanted more than a year of that discreet age. The little band of friends whose brotherhood he had so deeply enjoyed was broken up. Lamennais, as he felt painfully, was entering upon a path in which he could not follow; and between him and Lacordaire, though there was no real disagreement, there was a vague veil of separation—a something, a nothing—which yet detached them from each other; and few men have entered life so devoid of domestic ties as was this young man, whose heart positively hungered for love and the tenderer emotions. With a sadness and sense of isolation, which was only temporarily lightened by the society of M. Rio, he plunged into Germany. His interest in Christian art, no doubt, had originated in his friendship with his present companion, and had been largely cultivated by the journey which they had already taken together. During his solitary expeditions through France, although indignation against Vandalism had moved him more than pleasure, he had been inspired with an enthusiastic admiration for ancient architecture, and determination to defend the old churches at least in their external form, if it was not permitted to him to fight as a defender of the Church herself. And it was the architecture of Germany which now occupied him most—a rich and abundant subject; or rather this was his ostensible object, his argument to himself for quitting everything and plunging himself into that silence and solitude for which pensive youth so often feels a fantastic longing.

Rio, however, quitted him after a short time, having studies which called him to Munich; and then the solitude of the young traveller became very overwhelming. His heart is like a sea disturbed by storms, he tells us in his journal, quoting the words of St Augustine. It was when he had just fallen into this discouraging loneliness that chance led him to stay his wandering steps at the little town of Marbourg, on his way to Frankfort. There were few railways in those days, and travellers were compelled to make more frequent pauses, and form acquaintance with places out of the way. Here, however, he found an unexpected interest—a celestial friend awaiting him in the unknown place. Marbourg, small, dull, and chiefly Protestant, had been one of the shrines of the ancient worship, the city of St Elizabeth; and it was thus, all unawares, that the young enthusiast fell upon his true subject— the beautiful and varied history of those saintly lives which have been found more charming to the human race than any mythology, and by their mixture of actual humanity with religious truth, have done so much in all ages to promote and strengthen faith. According to the preface of his Life of St Elizabeth, it was on the saint's day that Montalembert arrived in Marbourg. He went to the church, his centre of interest in all such places, a noble Gothic building, stripped and cold, and dedicated to the Lutheran worship, but still retaining that inalienable beauty and majesty of form which

no neglect can fundamentally injure.   His first
note of this visit in his journal indicates rather
a deep and tender recollection of the fair young
sister whom he had lost some years before, and
who bore the name of the saint, than that
enthusiasm for the heavenly lady which was his
passion in the following years.   After he had
paid this first visit to the church, he went to a
bookseller's shop and asked if any life of St Elizabeth was to be found.   "The bookseller," says
M. Cochin, " made an expedition into his garret,
and brought out of it a pamphlet covered with
dust.   'Here is a life of her,' said the man, 'if
you take any interest in it ; it is never asked
for here, but I have one copy left, and here it
is.'"   By way of something to read, Montalembert took this little local publication with him,
when he set off by diligence to continue his
journey.   It was written by a Protestant, very
briefly and barely.   But the charm of that
beautiful romance of youthful self-devotion instantly began to assert its power.   The young
traveller in the lumbering German *schnellposte*
was moved to speedy enthusiasm ; his heart was
touched to its very depths, and his emotion was
brought to a climax when he remembered that
this day, on which he made acquaintance with
her life, was the very day dedicated to her in

the calendar of the Church. Instantly, with characteristic impetuosity, he resolved, according to his own words, to sacrifice to her "his fatigue and his hopes." Before he set out upon this journey he had vowed to himself that wherever a choice of things to do lay before him, he would choose that which was the most Catholic. He sprang out of the diligence when it came to its first halt, and carrying with him the poor little *brochure* which had thus filled his life all at once with a new hope and a new motive, took his place in the return coach, which was going back again to Marbourg, hoping to find out the poor little Catholic chapel of the place, and to hear mass there in celebration of the day. So far as this hope went, however, he was disappointed; there was no mass in the little neglected church. This chilled the impetuous young votary of the half-forgotten saint, who, melancholy alternative, took his way, when no mass was possible, in the rain—for even the weather declared itself against him—to the Lutheran superintendent, who was the author of the little book. Him he found to be a man "as intelligent as a Protestant could be ;" but does not seem to have derived very much information from him ; and next day went away considerably discouraged, and disposed to think that the return which he had made so eagerly to the deserted shrine had been in vain.

It would be curious now to see the little book, written by the man who was "as intelligent as was possible to a Protestant," which was the foundation of that beautiful medieval vision—tender and touching love - poem, and romance of religion, which filled the young man's life from this time until his first book was published. In the interval he wandered about like a chivalrous *minnesinger* of old—his harp slung at his back, yet his sword ever ready, murmuring everywhere that stately and sweet name of Elizabeth, the name of his lady in the skies. Such chivalrous and visionary passions are not rare in the Church of Rome, where men before now have been known to give themselves up, with a devotion strange to realise, to the purest, most visionary, and disinterested of attachments, the love of that holy and blessed Mary, who is not, as we think, a goddess to them, but something more sweet, more rare, more tender than any woman, while yet immeasurably above them—out of their reach, yet within it—the lady of their dreams. To us such devotion seems unreal and fantastical; but there are many instances in which it has been the inspiration of very tender and Christian souls shut out from any mortal love. And such the love of the holy Elizabeth became to Charles de Montalembert. All at once, in his sadness and loneliness, this divine lady came and smiled upon him, stirring herself in heaven as did the divine Beatrice when she came to Dante's aid :—

> " Donna e gentil nel ciel che si compiange,
>   Di questo impedimento ov io ti mando.
>   Sì che duro giudicio lassù frange."

We quote, from the introduction to the Life of St Elizabeth, the famous and beautiful description of the forlorn church, and the thoughts with which it inspired him :—

"On the 19th of November 1833 a traveller arrived at Marbourg, a town in the electorate of Hesse, situated upon the beautiful banks of the Lahn. He paused to examine the church, which was celebrated at once for its pure and perfect beauty, and because it was the first in Germany where the pointed arch prevailed over the round in the great renovation of art in the thirteenth century. This church bears the name of St Elizabeth, and it was on St Elizabeth's Day that he found himself within its walls. In the church itself, which, like the country, is now devoted to the Lutheran worship, there was no trace of any special solemnity, except that in honour of the day, and contrary to Protestant custom, it was open, and children were at play in it among the tombs. The stranger roamed through its vast, desolate, and devastated aisles, which are still young in their elegance and airy lightness. He saw placed against a pillar the statue of a young woman in the dress of a widow, with a gentle and resigned countenance, holding in one hand the model of a church, and with the other giving alms to a lame man. Further on, upon the naked altars, whence no priestly hand ever wiped the dust, he examined with interest ancient paintings on wood, well-nigh defaced, and carvings in relief, all broken, but both alike deeply impressed with the fresh and tender charm of Christian art. He saw among these pictures that of a terror-stricken girl showing to a crowned warrior her robe filled with roses; further on, this same warrior, stripping with violence the covering from his bed, is represented as finding Christ there, lying on the cross. Further on still, the two are shown tearing themselves with anguish from one another's arms; the lady is then depicted, fairer than in all the other representations, stretched on her bed of death midst weeping priests and nuns; and lastly, bishops exhume a coffin on which an emperor lays his crown. The tra-veller was told that these were events in the life of St Elizabeth, queen of that coun-try, who died on that day six hundred years ago in that very town of Marbourg, and lay buried in that very church. At the end of a dark sacristy he was shown the silver shrine, covered with sculpture, which had enclosed the relics of the saint, until one of her descendants, turned Protestant, had torn them from it and scattered them to the winds. Beneath the canopy of stone which once covered this shrine he saw that each step was deeply hollowed, and was told that these were the traces of countless pilgrims who once had come to kneel, but who for three centuries had come no more. He knew that there were certainly in that town some of the faithful and a Catholic priest, but neither mass nor any remembrance of the saint whose anniversary fell on that very day. The faith which had left its deep impress on the cold stone had left none upon human hearts.

"The stranger kissed the steps hollowed out by generations of the faithful, and retook his solitary course; but a sweet and sad recollection of the neglected saint, whose forgotten *fête* he had come, an unwitting pilgrim, to celebrate, left him no more. He undertook to study her life.

He ransacked in turn those rich stores of ancient learning which learned Germany offers in such profusion. Fascinated and charmed more every day by what he learned of her, the thought became little by little the guiding star of his course. After having exhausted the books and chronicles, and consulted the most neglected manuscripts, he was anxious, as the first of the old biographers of the saint had done, to examine localities and popular traditions. He went then from town to town, from castle to castle, from church to church, searching everywhere for traces of her who had ever been called in Catholic Germany the dear Saint Elizabeth.

"He tried in vain to visit her cradle at Presbourg, in far-off Hungary; but he could at least make some stay in the famous castle of Wartbourg, where she came when a child, and where she lived as a girl, and was married to a husband as tender and pious as herself. He could climb the rough paths by which she used to pass to distribute to the poor, her dearest friends, her never-failing alms. He followed her to Creuzburg, where first she became a mother; to the monastery of Reinhartsbräun, where at the age of twenty she was forced to part from her loved one, who went to die for the tomb of Christ; to

Bamberg, where she found a refuge from cruel persecution ; over the holy mountain of Andechs, the cradle of her race, where she offered up her wedding-dress, when, after the death of her dearly loved husband, she had become a wandering and exiled widow. At Erfurth he put to his lips the long glass which she had left in memory of herself to some humble sisters. Lastly, at Marbourg, where she consecrated the last days of her life to works of heroic charity, and where she died at the age of twenty-four, he returned to pray by her desecrated tomb, and to gather with pain and difficulty some remembrance of her from the mouths of a people who have renounced with the faith of their fathers the regard due to their benefactress."

From Marbourg the young pilgrim went to Frankfort; and there he found his old life clutching at him once more in a shadowy but painful way. On arriving at that town he found a letter from Lamennais, along with still another letter from the Pope, condemning once again that insubmissive priest. This was very grievous to Montalembert, who had, it would appear, for a moment extricated himself from this imbroglio, which was always growing darker and deeper.   In great distress and trouble of mind, all alone as he was, without any one to bias him, he discussed the whole matter over again within himself, feeling himself " obliged to examine the depths of his conscience and faith," in order to make sure what he should do.   The result of this examination was, that he made up his mind to advise Lamennais to submit once more.   For a long time after, this subject perplexed and filled him with pain.   Lacordaire wrote him incessant letters, begging him not to forsake the right way ; and the pious and distinguished Madame Swetchine, with whom he had made acquaintance in Paris, also wrote to him, urging and entreating him to be steadfast.   Against these letters came the plaints, the appeals, the remonstrances of Lamennais himself.   The young man was forced once more into the painful position of one whose heart attracts him to both sides, between two uncompromising opposites.   He staved off the pleadings of Lacordaire as he could, and with an affectionate subtilty which is touching in the circumstances, plied Lamennais, on the other hand, with all the arguments which Lacordaire had addressed to himself !   This one fact shows better than anything else could do the painfulness to a mind so affectionate of this position between two magnets, as it were, each of which drew him aside by turns. The agitation which existed at the same time among his friends, and their anxiety that he should come to a right decision on this matter, is well exemplified by a hasty and anxious letter, written in December by Albert de la Ferronays, in which he exclaims, " For heaven's sake, my friend, *force* yourself not to listen to the entreaties of M. de la Mennais!" A perfect storm of letters fell upon him at this crisis. Letters from Lamennais, full of suppressed rebellion and sentiments which began to shock and wound personally his young disciple; letters from Lacordaire, pleading, reasoning, appealing to his affection; and letters from Naples, and no doubt many other places, calling upon him to stand fast, in accents of painful alarm and uncertainty. Characteristic enough were the trifles by which Lamennais shook his own personal power. For one thing, he congratulated Montalembert on being a layman, and begged him to preserve at any price that blessed independence—a sentiment which was very painful to the feelings of so pious a Catholic. At another time he communicated the fact that he himself had given up all sacerdotal functions, no longer saying his daily mass, or fulfilling the special duties incumbent on a priest — a statement which made Montalembert's pen drop from his hand in horror as he recorded this terrible falling away. "For the first time," he cries, "I begin to fear freedom, if this is what it leads to." But when Lamennais, tired with so many remonstrances and contradictions, weary with the confused life into which these encyclical and Papal letters had thrown him, wrote hastily a kind of farewell to the friend who was no longer in full accord with him, curtly informing him that he should submit, but withdrawing in future from their intimate relationship, and adding the cruel words, "our paths are now separate," the sudden blow fell upon Montalembert like a thunderbolt. And nothing can show more clearly the profound sincerity and warmth of his affection for his "master," notwithstanding all their disagreements, than the letter which follows, published in Lamennais's correspondence, without name or date, but unquestionably his, and written in the very end of 1833 :—

"Some passages of your letter have been so cruel, so different from all that has ever passed between us, so different from the sentiments which I have always believed you to entertain towards me, that if they had not been in your handwriting I should never have imagined them to come from you.

"In announcing to me a step which is of so much importance for both of us, you refuse to tell me your motives; you say that 'you are about to commence a new life, but that you do not wish to communicate your ideas on this subject, because you desire to involve no one in your fate.' And you end by this phrase, which has filled me with consternation, 'We shall meet, I hope, on high; but we walk in two different paths on the earth.' I lose myself in endeavours to discover a reason for these terrible words. I venture to ask you what have you done with your memory? Can you have forgotten the intimate and tender friendship, paternal and filial, which has united us—I do not say since the beginning of the 'Avenir,' but still more especially since its end—since our journey to Italy—since our sojourn of S. Andrea delle Valle—since you gave me that pleasant name of 'son,' which I have always been so proud to bear? . . . What have I done to deserve so rapid and so harsh a change? How can you believe that a union so complete in the past, in the years which have been the most active and important in my life, and probably in yours also, should not have produced, at least for me, an enduring connection in the future. This thought, this hope, has always held the first place in my mind, and I cannot admit for an instant the possibility of giving it up. . . . I belong to you altogether; and now that my conscience is no longer oppressed with doubt as to the direction in which you may be thrown, I am ready to obey you at your first word. To be able to associate myself with you, and to find a sacred duty in following and waiting upon you, will be for me consolation and happiness."

But while Montalembert made this passionate declaration of personal attachment and devotion, he was unshaken in the gradual resolution he was forming not to allow himself to be drawn away by a single step from his attitude of submission towards the Church; and the reader will feel that he has travelled round to the other side of the globe, or rather that the solid globe has turned with him, bringing antipodal night suddenly into the warmth of sunrise, when he reads the following brief response, which has in it a certain excusable asperity of impatience, and which was written in answer to three anxious letters addressed to him by the family of de la Ferronays, in which Albert, Pauline, and

Alexandrine, each after their fashion, had pleaded with and entreated him not to allow himself to be led away. The reply is dated from Munich the 3d January 1834, and must have been written only a few days after the letter just quoted.

" I confess that I have been much surprised by reading the reflections which my letter from Frankfort has called forth from you, all three. I must have expressed myself very badly if I have left you to suspect for a moment that I should not exactly follow the course you advise me. It appears to me, however, that I told you expressly that I was going to Munich, and that if I had for a moment thought of going to Paris, it was for the purpose of using my feeble influence with M. de Lamennais, to turn him from all idea of resistance. All the excellent thoughts which you express with so much affection, goodness, and that true eloquence which comes from the heart, have been my very sentiments; and there is not a word in your letters which does not exactly agree with all that I have thought and wished since I read the fatal brief of October 5th. There is not even a word in them which I have not already said or written to M. de Lamennais to persuade him to act as I did

—to retire from the field, bow himself under the severe hand of God, and await humbly and submissively the accomplishment of a higher will. But, strange to say, and I hesitate to tell it to you, M. de Lamennais has shown himself wounded by my counsel, although I gave it with more tenderness, solicitude, and anxiety than I should have shown to any other living being. His answer proves only too well how much my dissent from him has grieved him, and that his heart is changed towards me. I should never have believed it, and I do not think I have deserved it. However, he has taken the part I advised."

This seems to have been almost the first time that Montalembert avowed his disappointment with the friend to whom he had been so faithful. Lamennais rarely appears again in the journal. There is a passing groan of regret and grief over the "Paroles d'un Croyant;" but fortunately another interest had come into the young man's life. In the very midst of his distress, while he declares himself "miserable" at the fall of his master, he introduces to us, as it were with the other hand, his new love. The grandeur of the middle ages attracted and consoled him. "If I could but forget my political hopes!" he cries. In that case his religious studies might yet afford to him happiness and peace.

There is, however, another want and void in his life which begins to make itself felt, and is expressed with a simplicity and *naïveté* which make the reader smile. We doubt whether an Englishman would, even in the sacred retirement of his journal, make his plaint so simply and openly. At intervals through all his young life, his sense of solitude seems to have recurred to Montalembert, weighing him to the very ground. There were circumstances which specially forced this upon his mind in the spring of 1834. Albert de la Ferronays was about to be married to his beloved Alexandrine; and his friend Rio, too, was on the eve of marriage. It was this later event which forced from him the plaints which appear in his journal during his stay in Munich. All at once, out of his troubles with Lamennais, and his conflict with himself, his mind veers round to a different, very different subject, and he bursts forth into a melancholy cry. He feels his position "miserably inferior" to that of Rio, the bridegroom; and with whimsical wretchedness he proceeds to record that he dares not speak to a pretty girl when he meets one; that it is painful to him to see a beautiful young wife even in the street—especially in such a place as Munich, where lovemaking is carried on in the street! For what has he to do with love? At twenty-four he has begun to lose the power of feeling; he has lost even the years that belong to love, and it is a pain to him to hear its name. "I have never been able to touch the heart of any woman," he says, with a misery which is perfectly real, but which it is difficult not to smile at. His "inferiority" went to his heart; and it was with a sigh of profound sadness, and something like mortification, that he turned from the sight of that happiness which he envied, to throw himself into the service of his saintly lady Elizabeth. She was his substitute for the earthly loves which filled other men's lives with happiness. "She," he exclaims in a moment of effusion, "is my only friend."

While he was at Munich he went upon a pious pilgrimage to Andechs, where his saint had gone before him, and where she had given her wedding-dress as an offering. With enthusiasm he describes the homely procession of the pilgrims. They were chiefly poor people, belonging to the peasant class, and full of that simple yet high-toned piety which has a charm of frankness and simplicity unknown to more lofty worshippers. His piety as a gentleman and a foreigner made as deep an impression upon them. "I don't know what country you are of," one of them said to him, "but you are a good Catholic, and you are my brother." This gave a passing pleasure to the heart of the solitary young wanderer; but he is always ready to recur to the subject of his loneliness. It is a string which the mere passing breeze touches into melancholy vibration. His heart is empty and his life is a failure, he says—*une vie manquée*. While he was thus sighing his heart out, Albert at Naples, in the delightful foolishness of his betrothal, was asking Alexandrine for a ring on which *C'est pour la vie* was inscribed; and was refused with the smiling, tender response, *C'est trop courte, la vie!* All these sweet follies came pouring upon young Montalembert in the happy lover's letters; and on the other side of him was Rio, to whom he felt so inferior! No wonder that he felt his lonely life to be *manquée*—he who had never yet been able to touch a woman's heart!

After his stay in Munich, where he studied in the public libraries, and pursued his search after details of the life of his beloved saint, he went into Thuringia, which was her country, or rather the country of her husband, where she had spent almost the whole of her life. In one obscure and small place here, he found the original MS. of her life, ornamented with miniatures. At Erfurt he visited the Ursuline Convent, which had been one of her favourite resorts, and where the room which she had occupied was shown to him, and a glass which she had used, and which all the girls at the school (though Protestants) drink out of on the day of her *fête*. He approached this sacred glass reverently to his lips. At Eisenach, which is the next point noted, family recollections of a tender kind united themselves with his pursuits. It was one of the places at which he had stayed for a day or two with his mother and sister, five years before, not long before the death of Elise. Looking through the books of the hotel he saw his own name written there, and immediately all the circumstances of his former visit came back to his mind. One of the waiters, too, recognised him, and recollected his sister—a fact which touched the traveller deeply. The man spoke with tears in his eyes, of the fair fading young creature, whose appearance had made an impression upon him; and Montalembert, it is evident, opened his heart forthwith to this humble sympathiser, telling him how lonely he was; for he records,—"The waiter says he is better off than I am; he is not alone in the world." At Eisenach he spent the anniversary of his father's death, a day which overwhelmed him all the more that the place was sternly Protestant, and no priest was there from whom he could ask a mass for the soul of the departed. The Protestantism of the district altogether was a sad stumbling-block and trouble to him. The Reformation had not only obliterated the dear St Elizabeth, but had substituted in her place a substantial figure, whose very name is obnoxious to all good Catholics. Montalembert found the burly form of Martin Luther established in the Wartburg, reigning in the guide-books, and sought after by all those profane and chattering pilgrims who call themselves tourists. And it is easy to enter into the feelings with which he, a real pilgrim, with a true and reverential love for the distant past, took his solitary way to the old castle where his saint had lived, in the enforced company of a fluttering and noisy Protestant crowd, who went to gaze at the stains made on the wall by Luther's inkstand, and to laugh with nineteenth century flippancy at the Reformer's devil. Luther's inkstand and his demon and himself were alike sickening to the young Catholic, an effect which indeed the company of a crowd of tourists was of itself enough to produce. He went about with his heart full, avoiding as much as he could the noisy stream of people, trying to find some traces of the older and sweeter inhabitant. But very few were left; "everything," he exclaims indignantly, "is Luther!" As the tourists went wandering up and down, filling the ancient place with voices and laughter and vulgar din of to-day, Montalembert gathered some white roses and forget-me-nots—"fleurs de Sainte- Elizabeth"—a soft recollection of nature which did something to console him. But he tells us that the Wartburg was to him like another Holy Land in the possession of the infidels—a strong metaphor, which, however, is very comprehensible, and which the warmest Protestant, with a heart susceptible to human sympathies, will forgive to the melancholy and solitary young wanderer. In the entire district, which to him was sanctified by the name of Elizabeth, there was not one single soul who could understand his sentiments, or enter into his half-pious, half-romantic devotion. In the library of Eisenach he found some materials that proved of use to him ; but the librarian, too, was a Protestant, incapable of understanding what he sought or why he sought it. In short, this holy land of medieval Catholicism was the holy land of the Reformation too, and Luther had superseded Elizabeth even in the hospital which her charity had founded.

From Eisenach Montalembert returned to Marbourg, where he resumed his beloved studies in the place where he had first learned to know his saint. But the June days were long, and passed slowly with nothing but this study to enliven them; and the little German town, full of Protestants, had all the strangeness without any of the excitement of a new place. There was, indeed, the beautiful church of St Elizabeth, full of old records in stone, and old pictures of her forgotten life; but none to whom he could speak of his subject, or who could give him the moral support of their sympathy. The Lutheran superintendent who had written the *brochure* which revealed that celestial lady to her new adorer, moved, no doubt, by the sight of the interest he had evoked, began to think of a new edition of his little book, and shut up his lips in consequence, refusing to communicate any further information; and when we reflect what the thoughts must have been in Montalembert's mind while he wandered through the beautiful forsaken aisles of the old church, or by the riverside under the acacias, it will not be difficult to understand the visionary depression which weighed him down. A waif and stray upon the earth, as he must have felt himself, without any strong link of domestic love to hold him to one place more than another in this dreary world—blown this way and that by gusts of opinion—now clutched at by Lamennais's impatient hand, now pushed back by Lacordaire — censured by the Pope, yet in his heart submitting to the Pope,—with room for all of them in his warm affections, if only they would have permitted him to love them without insisting on agreement as well. And Rio and Albert, one on each side, insulting his solitude with their happiness, with raptures which rent his heart, and which, it appeared to him, he could never share !

All these miseries fled, however, to the winds one morning when his solitary chamber door was opened, and Lacordaire looked in. This unexpected visit filled him with happiness as unexpected. Even the discussions which followed, the long arguments, the reconsideration once more, and over and over again, of the old story, were changed—by the fact that they could be discussed in person, *a quattr'occhi* —from pain into pleasure. "He came to me at the tomb of St Elizabeth to persuade me," says Montalembert. "I was displeased with my friend, because he had taken another way from mine, and had pronounced himself more publicly and decisively. I was even bold enough to reproach him with his apparent forgetfulness of those liberal opinions with which we had been both set on fire." And "it was then," he adds, "that my eyes, at first distracted and irritable, but soon and always after, wet with the tears of everlasting gratitude, penetrated into the very depths of that generous soul." There is nothing, however, of these discussions in the journal, but only a burst of delight at his friend's arrival—delight which throws a reflection upon Marbourg itself, and the Lahn, and all the surrounding scenery. With Lacordaire by his side, our young solitary found Marbourg as fine as Salzbourg. He took his friend to all his haunts—to the cathedral, which he admired with enthusiasm—and no doubt to all those promenades of the little town which had been so dull to him; and with what effusion of the heart he poured forth all his griefs, all his restless longings for happiness, all his doubts and difficulties, into that attentive ear! He "told everything" to Lacordaire, and was consoled.

We must not, however, linger too long upon

the details which reveal the young man to us day by day. He continued during the autumn his loving pilgrimage to the places made memorable and holy by the residence or charities of his saint, and began, in the intervals of his wanderings, the beautiful book which was the result of so much loving labour. In the begin- of winter he recrossed the Alps; and we find him again immediately after, with that delighful difference in the presentment which is made when the hand of a friend takes up the pencil which has dropped from his own, in the little ideal household, where every day's history is an idyl, of Albert de la Ferronays, at Pisa. On the threshold of this charming picture we pause to quote a letter from that young and happy bridegroom—who had already, however, been attacked by the cruel disease which killed him. By this the reader will perceive what were the kind of commissions with which these ardent young friends charged each other. The letter is dated from Pisa, the 5th November 1834 :—

" Dear friend, before you leave Florence will you make a pilgrimage for me to Santa Maria Novella? In the first or second chapel to the right of the high altar, behind the altar, you will find a tomb in black marble, surmounted by a group representing the Virgin Mary surrounded by angels. Three years ago I went often to pray there, and I have always retained the feeling that I owe my happiness to the prayers which I left behind that altar; for it was in that year that, after leaving Florence, I met Alexandrine in Rome. I am superstitious, because I am happy. Pray there, then, for yourself—ask for a similar happiness. All is posible to God, and He grants everything to faith. Then ask for health for me. Is it wrong? After so much happiness should not I be able to bear some suffering? The will of God be done! but I hope that my prayers will not displease Him. You understand? Pray much for me there. . . .

"Try, my dear friend, not to leave Lucca till noon, because I am forbidden to go out before two o'clock, and I want to go and meet you; unless, indeed, it was your intention to leave so early as to be here before my hour for going out. In that case it is very different. Don't delay a moment. I long too much to see you."

When we remember that this bridegroom, so ideally happy, so good, so young, was even at that moment entering the valley of the shadow of death, there is something heart-rending in his mixture of human longings and gentle youthful submission. "Is it wrong?" His friend, we may be sure, fulfilled his commission to the letter; and many a pious young Catholic no doubt since then has sought the black tomb, with its crown of angels, to breathe that prayer which is the most wistful and touching utterance of the human soul—that prayer for the dead which Rome authorises, and which nature clings to, whether it be a duty or a sin—for the gentle spirit of Albert. Strangely enough, poor nature, half instructed, cheats herself as usual in those longing supplications, and utters her cries of love for those who have least need of them, for the predestined angels whose heaven the veriest sceptic dares not doubt.

On the 10th November, Madame Albert de la Ferronays, the beloved Alexandrine who is the heroine of the ' Recit d'une Sœur,' announces thus the arrival of her husband's friend :—

"Montal arrived at seven in the evening. Albert is so happy! We rushed to meet him upon the stair. He has told me several times since that the cordiality with which I received him surprised, but put him at his ease. He had been a little frightened by the idea of finding me established here, a third party between

Albert and him. But how could I have received him otherwise than cordially? Albert loves him with a friendship such as I never saw before."

From this date for about two months the diary of the young wife is full of this cherished friend. They went together to the Campo Santo in the moonlight; they took long walks together, Albert sometimes taking refuge in the carriage which followed them. And it was with Montalembert that Alexandrine, still trembling between her old Lutheranism and the faith of her husband, went to the Christmas midnight mass at the cathedral, when Albert was not able to go. "How grieved I was to go without Albert!" she says; "he who would have been so happy there. He was ill, however, and ought to have gone to bed; but when we came back he was still up, waiting for us with tea ready, so resigned, so light-hearted and charming!"

And never was there housemate more agreeable than the young visionary, the solitary enthusiast of Marbourg, the politician of Paris. He made himself the servant as well as the friend of the young pair; he took upon him all the active offices for which Albert's weakness disqualified him; he carried their letters to the post; he went and bought chestnuts for them, and no doubt other necessaries; he added a new charm of genial conversation, and all the novelty of his travels, to the lovers' *tête-à-tête*, which was never dull, but which nevertheless was all the sweeter for this pleasant interruption. In the morning Albert went up-stairs to the apartment which his friend occupied overhead, and spent the morning with him. In the afternoons they went out together, always with the carriage close by, in case Albert should be fatigued. In the evening after their gay dinner, which perhaps was not splendid, for none of the party were rich, "Montal" read to them— sometimes legends of the saints, and among others those associated with the life of St Francis of Assisi, no doubt the delightful and *naïve* Fioretti di San Francesco. Once or twice he read short extracts from his manuscript of St Elizabeth, which delighted them, and filled the young pair with a gentle pride in their friend. "How he loves this St Elizabeth!" cries Alexandrine, in one of her letters. "He collects the smallest, the most minute details about her. He told me the other day a story of a knight who wore the colours of a saint who had appeared to him in a dream. . . .

What do you think of the life we lead? For my part I love it. We subscribe to the library in Leghorn, and our tables are covered with reviews, with journals (these last for Montal), with Walter Scott's novels for Albert, and other books of all kinds for him and for me." Then she sang to the two delighted young men the German airs, of which "Montal had made a delightful collection during his journey in Germany." "It is so delightful, so singular, so good," says Albert, "for our three natures, to let the days flow together, without any bondage of society, in perfect intimacy, having no ties but those of the heart." We will quote two other simple vignettes of this delightful episode in the life of the three friends; and the reader who knows the scene in which it occurred will have little difficulty in surrounding the three young figures with that still background of half-deserted Pisa, with all its tall palaces, and the grass growing in its streets, and Arno running brown between the majestic lines of houses on either bank. Pisa was in its mild winter flutter of society; and the pleasant humility and simplicity of the life which poor gentlefolks are able to live in scraps of great Italian palaces, finding to their own surprise that poverty is practicable and even pleasant, rises before us

like a breath from the past. The first of these
delightful little sketches is dated Tuesday, 13th
January 1835 :—

"We all went to the Cascine, then (which
amused us much) we all went to order a bonnet
for me. At dinner Albert suddenly took the
resolution of going to a ball which was to be
given that evening, but which we had all three
declined. I resisted, fearing that it might do
him harm ; but he insisted, and ending by saying, 'Je le veux.' He told my maid to prepare
everything, and by degrees I allowed myself to
be persuaded into the pleasant annoyance of
making myself as pretty as possible (*'je me
laissai faire la douce violence'*). This occupied
me entirely for two hours. To make the joke
complete, we forced Montal to go with us. We
had hard work to succeed in this, for he had
nothing to put on. Albert lent him almost
everything. Then it was necessary to get a
shoemaker for him, and a hairdresser to cut his
hair. All this amused us immensely ; and the
end of all, which made us laugh more than all
the rest, was that, recollecting all at once that
we had no servant, we took the shoemaker's
boy with us in that capacity to go with us to
the ball ! "

Albert adds, with all the glee of an invalid breaking rules, the day after this ceremony, "Yesterday I forced my wife to go to a ball. *Idem*, I dragged Montal there, and after an hour of moderate satisfaction, we returned to take tea at home. My little Alex," adds the young husband, "was charming in her pretty blue dress, and with her diamonds." How attractive is this soft boyish, childish gaiety, the little bright scene full of delightful laughter, among so many shadows of closely-gathering darkness !

This charming little society, however, had to be broken up before long. On the 15th January Alexandrine joined her husband up-stairs in Montal's rooms for the first and last time, while he packed his possessions before his journey. Here is the description of this "dernière soirée chez Montal" :—

"He had got bewildered in the midst of his trunks, his books, and his papers. I looked at his books a little ; they had almost all a religious purport, but there were also many legends and national histories. I helped him to pack, and while we did so we discussed religious subjects a little. He read to me in triumph a fine passage from Alphonso de Liguori upon the worship of the Holy Virgin, in which I did not yet believe, and persuaded me to burn Father Clement (a book which was supposed an antidote to Catholicism, lent to me by some Protestant friends, but which had a totally different effect from that which it was intended to produce). Then we went down-stairs, still very happy. Montal made me sing a quantity of romances and national airs, which he had collected in his journeys. Among them was a charming German hymn, the words translated from St Bernard (*Jesus wie süs, wer dein gedenkt*), and which said that nothing was so sweet as to think of Jesus, nothing so delightful as His presence. Montal made me sing it over and over, though at first he had thought it was almost a profanation to allow me to sing it at all. He was astonished to hear that I sang it with an expression approaching, he said, to that of three pious girls at Ratisbonne, who sang it while they worked."

This amusing bit of intolerance did not affront Alexandrine, who was very nearly converted into as good a Catholic as either of her audience, and who all through her beautiful young life seems to have been as humbly conscious of the infirmity of her Protestantism as could be desired. The three sat up together till half-past two in the morning, enjoying to the utmost the sad delights of their last evening together. "He wept when he left us," says Alexandrine, "and regretted this good family life, as he called it, which we have lived together, and to which he had grown so thoroughly accustomed." The very letter in which this account of the leave-taking is contained had to be retarded, as the Italian maid would not go out in the evening to post it, and the young couple felt their want of servants, "now that we no longer have Montalembert." He went away in bad weather, with a sympathetic accompaniment of rain and cloudy skies; and the first letters his friends wrote to him are full of lamentations over his loss. "You have no idea of the void which you have left in our poor little *home*" (the latter word in English), writes Albert. "We regret you much, very much" (*beaucoup, beaucoup*), says Alexandrine; "and I don't know if we shall be able to resume the cheerfulness which we had before you arrived, for at dinner and at tea there is always a vacant place, which recalls sadly the excellent friend who filled it so well. . . . Keep us informed," she adds, "very exactly of the fate of our dear St Elizabeth; you know how much interest we take in her; and you who write so rapidly, write to us everything about yourself, as illegibly and hastily as you like—we shall always be able to read it."   .

Thus terminated his share in the idyl of his friends. His own idyl was still some little distance off. He returned to Paris to take his seat in the House of Peers, as he now approached the end of his twenty-fifth year, the age at which a peer of France attained his political majority ; and after the brilliant false start of the 'Avenir,' and all the troubles it brought in its train, to begin seriously his public life, and make his appearance in the world with the gravity of a man.

CHAPTER IX.

THE COMMENCEMENT OF PUBLIC LIFE.

MONTALEMBERT returned from his wanderings in the year 1835, and settled in Paris. His most intimate and cherished friends were now collected in the place which is so dear to every Frenchman. Lacordaire, once more chaplain of the Visitandines, had already become known as a great preacher by his " Conferences "—a series of Lenten sermons—at the College Stanislas; and in the Lent of this year reached to the height of his fame in Nôtre Dame, where all Paris rushed to hear him—the archbishop himself occupying his episcopal place, and all that was best in France crowding round the pulpit. It would be difficult to exaggerate the effect which these wonderful discourses produced in France. They took up in a more effectual way the echoes of that religious excitement which had been called forth by the passionate chivalry of the 'Avenir,' and moved the mass of society as no preacher had done for more than a century. They took away the reproach of religion, if we may use such words. Neither Lacordaire himself, nor the friends who supported him, could be any longer contemptuously stigmatised as *gens de la Sacristie*. And any spectator who may have witnessed the Conferences of preachers much less notable than Lacordaire, which still were held within the last few years at the same sacred season in Nôtre Dame, will be very well able to understand the contagion of pious enthusiasm, and the emotion and prepossession towards Christian faith (to speak of no more solemn impression) which must have been produced by these immense assemblies. The new society of St Vincent de Paul, just formed by Ozanam, in all its beginning of fervour, formed the nucleus of the audience, and around this little phalanx the crowd surged, daily growing greater. "You too," cried Montalembert many years afterwards, in generous indignation, appealing to the recollections of those who had forsaken their first love—"you too swelled these crowds, intoxicated with eloquence and enthusiasm, you who now profess to doubt the existence of that which you have forgotten or betrayed." The whole gay

world of Paris was moved to its centre by this
new influence; and though it may be true that
many centres of real and humble piety are to
be found at all times even in the most corrupt
society—a fact which we believe devoutly—
yet it is certain that at this moment those centres of piety were of a kind more remarkable,
and calculated to catch the eye and attention,
than is at all common in the world. Madame
Swetchine, noble, wise, and pious, endowed with
all that power of personal influence which tells
so much upon society, gave to the religious
party that wonderful advantage in France, a
salon, where wit and genius, and all that was
most socially attractive, removed piety into a
region where it was unassailable by the profane
wits of *esprit fort* and scoffing philosopher;
and the young men who attached themselves to
her were all men rising into note, eminent in
literature and eloquence, and destined to greatness in the public service. There was in this
sympathetic society much that was congenial
to Montalembert. Except in so far as Lamennais was concerned, who fortunately was but
for a short time in Paris, he was in full accord
with all his companions. And even the fret of
that painful connection seems to have terminated
during this season. Lacordaire was in his

immediate neighbourhood ; Madame Swetchine gave him the affectionate reception of a mother; and Rio had established himself at St Germains, within reach. Accordingly he settled down in Paris, and took up seriously the composition of his Life of St Elizabeth, for which he had collected materials so conscientiously and carefully. With his books, his papers, his collections of MSS. and legends round him, he gave himself up to the laborious life which was congenial and natural to his mind, sweetened by that perpetual intercourse with his friends which was still dearer. At the very same time another book of kindred character, the 'Poesie de l'Art Chrétien,' was likewise growing into being. And "in a charming house near the terrace, the windows of which commanded a delightful view over the country," Rio read to Montalembert, "the most sympathetic and the most constant of our visitors," parts of his manuscript,—"those portions which I knew would be in harmony with his personal impressions, which were not always the same as my own." Here the imagination pauses on a distinct and delightful picture which presents itself like an illustration to our story. That terrace of St Germains, so full of historical recollections, with the deep coolness of the summer woods behind, and Seine running softly by upon its immemorial pilgrimage ; here, in this storied seclusion, from which the *Grand Monarque* fled to escape the constant view of those towers of St Denis, which recalled to him his future tomb, and where the last of the Stuart kings hid his unhappy head, and brooded over his lost throne,—these two young men compared their recollections, exchanged their literary confidences, and together, in the fire and fervour of their youth, opened the great grave of the past, and brought out from it many a wonder, rich and strange, which the times had forgotten. It was the renaissance of all that beautiful and lofty art which, up to that time, had been buried in neglected old churches, and allowed to crumble in broken-down cloisters. All our present ideas in respect to art have, more or less, taken colour, though we knew it not, from those researches and readings. For France especially it was the reopening of one splendid chapter of her history, the disinterring of her middle ages from their dusty and sordid tomb.

While thus, however, our young author laboured to "vindicate the Christian ideal in history," as his friend did in art, other duties also occupied his thoughts. He had taken his place in the House of Peers on attaining the age of twenty-five; and although he was not allowed to vote until he was thirty, his Parliamentary career as a speaker immediately began. It was the year in which the infernal machine of Fieschi was directed against the life of Louis Philippe—an occasion which would have roused all the sympathies of the nation had not the Government of the moment done their best to quench the good feeling of the people by that fatal inclination to coercion which seems to affect all parties alike in France the moment that power is put into their hands. The Government of July, created by journalism and individual opinion, succumbed to this apparently irresistible tradition; and after the attempt on the king, presented to the Parliament the so-called laws of September, entitled by their framers, not " repressive," but " suppressive" of all discussion which should affect the person of the king, the rights of the reigning house, and the constitution of the country. Not only in newspapers, but in the theatres and *in pictures*, was any discussion of these three subjects, or—discussion in art being impossible—any attempt to shake their authority, forbidden under penalties " intended to make all escape impossible." It was in opposition, but in vain opposition, to this law that Montalembert made his first speech as a member of the Chamber; and no better illustration could be given of the sense in which he had made his submission to the Pope's sentence, which we have already treated at such length. He submitted to that sentence with perfect docility and good grace, so far as it affected the 'Avenir' and his own movements; but he did not pretend to adopt, nor did he ever feel it necessary to assent to, the opinion of the Holy See in respect to the liberty of the press. Thus after three years, which had been rendered aimless, and filled with much vexation and annoyance, in consequence of his personal obedience to the commands of the Church, the young politician, leaving that ground which it had cost him so much to hold, but without for a moment giving up his submission as a Catholic, stood up in impassioned defence of that principle which Pope Gregory had pronounced accursed, but which Montalembert never ceased to think of the highest importance to true freedom. Nothing could better illustrate how far his submission went, and where it stopped absolutely short.

We cannot give any *résumé* of the speech itself, for we are now at the commencement of his public life, which is full of speeches, and which would soon occupy much more space than is at our command did we enter into it in detail; but we may note the effect which, according to various writers, his appearance made upon the Chamber of Peers—an assembly unaccustomed to the fervour and warmth and young eloquence which thus suddenly burst forth among them. All agree in giving to the new orator a quite exceptional position. The French Chamber of Peers never possessed the dignity or authority of our own House of Lords; but it partook of the nullity and formal blank of powerlessness which make our Upper House the terror of aspiring politicians, and had, besides, a character of artificiality and uncertainty such as is unknown to any of our institutions. It was a creation, against the instincts of the times, and only waiting the day when the popular forces should be strong enough to pull it to pieces. In the midst of this artificial existence, the voice of the young peer, who was a real man of his time, undeniable in life and fact, struck the half-dead Chamber with such a sense of actual existence as it had rarely felt before. "When he re-appeared in the Chamber," says Sainte-Beuve, "he had the right to say anything, to dare anything, so long as he retained that elegance of aspect and diction which never forsook him. He could utter with all freedom the most passionate pleadings for that liberty which was the only excess of his youth. He could develop without interruption those absolute theories which from another mouth would have made the Chamber shiver, but which pleased them from his. He could even give free course to his mordant and incisive wit, and make personal attacks with impunity upon potentates and ministers. In one or two cases the Chancellor called him to order for form's sake ; but the favour which attends talent carried everything before it. His bitterness—and he was sometimes bitter— from him seemed almost amenity, the harshness of the meaning being disguised by the elegance of his manner and his perfect good grace." "It was," adds M. Nettement, "a sight full of interest to see this ardent, enthusiastic, impetuous young man rise in the midst of the Chamber of Peers, composed almost entirely of the relics of past conditions of society—men grown grey in public business, worn out with politics, and among whom experience had destroyed enthusiasm—and disturb with the accents of an impassioned voice the decent calm, the elegant reserve, and the polite conventionality, full of knowledge of things and men (*savoir et savoir vivre*), yet somewhat cold, of their habitual discussions—as he vindicated, in the name of new generations and of the future, the rights and interests of that religion which was said to have no partisans but old men, and no life but in the past."

His actual Parliamentary *début* was thus made in defence of the liberty of the press, as his first premature appearance in that assembly had been in defence of the liberty of teaching. Freedom, whether in one particular of national life or in another, was the perpetual refrain, the burden of his life. "I do not pretend," he said, " to constitute myself the champion of the liberty of the press or of any other liberty— they have no need of my defence. Liberty, I am deeply convinced, has become the inalienable inheritance of France. . . . What I am about to defend by attacking this projected enactment is rather social order, which is gravely threatened by an unforeseen overturn of the ideas and habits which have long reigned amongst us—and the Government of July, which is endangered in its popularity and honour, in its just and salutary influence, by a number of violent measures, of which the present is the most serious."

Thus he began his Parliamentary career in

opposition.   It was his natural place and tendency.   That he had candour and nobleness of
mind sufficient to overcome this natural inclination when any government, however displeasing
to him, originated measures which he believed
for the good of the people, will be abundantly
demonstrated in his later life.   But at the same
time all the impulses of nature tended to separate him from the side of power.   The alerts
and surprises of political assault and criticism
had a great deal more attraction for him than
the monotony of empire could ever have had ;
but the opposition which he thus began, and
which he carried on more or less during all the
period in which political life was possible to
him, was of a kind little known in France and
much misunderstood.   He opposed the Government of Louis Philippe from no desire to bring
in another government, or to prepare another
revolution.   He was not hostile to the throne,
though he thus set himself to criticise and censure its action.   He was indeed serving the
throne after his fashion, and more truly, more
wisely, than those who advised the coercions he
opposed.   It was the Government which he defended against itself, against the evil agencies
which it was bringing into being for its own
destruction.   In short, he was the representa-

tive, and almost the only representative, of constitutional opposition, without *arrière pensée*
or hostile motive, in France. But this position
was one little understood by, nay, all but incomprehensible to his countrymen. It came to him
from his English blood, from his grandfather's
library, from the habit of a much reflective
mind, and of a generous impatient spirit, to which
wrong was intolerable. The time indeed came
when even this generously impatient soul learned
for one critical moment to submit to expediency, and to follow the leading of circumstances;
but that time was still distant : and in opposition
a man may hold by absolute rules of right and
wrong which would be impracticable to a ruler,
or at least which no ruler has had the strength
of mind to attempt to carry out in practice.
He did all that man could do to familiarise his
country with the existence of a loyal and law-
loving opposition. But to most Frenchmen it
still seems easier to retire into proud seclusion,
or to turn aside into conspiracy, than to work
at actual government from the wrong side.
Montalembert has left at least a tradition behind
him of this noble and self-denying *rôle*, but we
fear that at most times he alone constituted all
his party, and that even he has scarcely made
its principles understood.

We may pause here, however, to note among the many beautiful aspects of his character the one referred to by Sainte-Beuve in the words above quoted, and which formed the one jarring note amid so much harmony.   Now, and at all times, there was in his fine and melodious nature a harsher vibration, as of some chord which had been overstrained, and gave forth a sharp discord when any unwary touch came upon it.   "He was sometimes bitter," says Sainte-Beuve; and this sharpness was not confined to his public appearances.   There are indications in the 'Récit d'une Sœur,' that even his most admiring friends sometimes suffered by this unforeseen and sudden shaft, which would fall like a flash of lightning out of a serene sky, in the midst of the warmest and most affectionate intercourse.   Even the praise of Albert de la Ferronays, "Tu es ni froid ni railleur pour moi," shows a consciousness of this alarming quality; and there is one mild little plaint made by the gentle Alexandrine, which shows a wound.   "I have been a little hurt by the terms 'dissipated and dangerous' which you used in speaking of my life before my marriage," she says.   "This wounds me on account of my parents.   Dear and good friend, it seems to me that you are sometimes too severe for this poor world." It is very seldom that this sharp and harsh vibration makes itself heard, but it does come now and then, a tone, an accent, over in a moment, yet full of the power to sting.

In the beginning of his career, however, Montalembert made little employment of this prodigious weapon in public warfare. He was too immensely in earnest, too exalted in thought and style as yet, to trust to a gibe. The chivalrous character which distinguished his whole life is very notable in his various public appearances at this early stage of his career, while as yet he was "pricking o'er the plain," a gentle knight ready to answer any call of the oppressed, but not bound to any special enterprise. His next subject was Poland. The Emperor Nicholas had abolished the charter granted to the Poles by his predecessors, and their constant sympathiser and champion in France immediately took up their cause. We will not attempt, as we have already said, to give an account of his early speeches; but one or two extracts may be of use to the reader, as showing the various sides of his character as well as of his opinions,—his power of sympathy in the most different causes, the real insight which we can understand and acknowledge in so many cases, and the other class of sentiments, which were as truly a part of his mind, which we can neither agree in nor understand.   Here, for instance, is an instructive passage, showing once more his high opinion of England, and at the same time throwing a curious light upon a state of affairs now, alas! come to an end. To stimulate his own country by the example of her insular neighbour, was always one of his favourite desires.   His object on this occasion was to call forth a public expression of French sympathy for the Poles.

"Far be it from me to embarrass in the smallest degree the King's Government, or to interpose a movement of unreflecting violence into its policy.   But each one has an individual part to play.   Let the executive power retain a diplomatic freedom and reserve if it will, but let the Legislature be permitted to make a frank and sincere avowal of national sentiments, and the firm and decided expression of national opinion.   This is its right, its duty, and its special mission.   It owes the accomplishment of this duty not only to the country, but to the world.   In that unequal division of the rights and duties of public life which has been made among the nations of the earth, those who are most richly endowed with these crowning posses-

sions are bound, as the rich are bound towards
the poor, to make up for that unjust partition
by beneficent sympathy, and by constant interest in outraged and enslaved nations. In a
period like ours, when the fusion of different
races becomes daily more complete, the obliga-
tion which is imposed by humanity is not less
required by wise policy. In this lies the glorious privilege of free speech (*tribunes libres*);
it is the crown of political existence. What is
it that has raised the British Parliament to so
high a degree of popularity and moral influence
in Europe ? Is it not because for more than a
century no grave event has happened in any
country without finding an echo there ? Is it
not because no right has been oppressed, no treaty
broken anywhere, without a discussion on both
sides of the question before the Peers and Commons of England, whose assemblies have thus
become, in the silence of the world, a sort of
tribunal where all the great causes of humanity
are pleaded, and where opinion pronounces those
formidable judgments which sooner or later are
always executed ? "

After this intelligent and eloquent description
of one attitude of power—of the free and full and
(in those days) sympathetic discussions of Eng-

land, here is a picture of another attitude, and a totally different kind of moral influence. It is contained not in a speech, but in an article published in the 'Univers' (at that time, be it remembered, a totally different paper from the one which now bears that name), and is devoted to the consideration of events which made a great noise in their day, though they have well-nigh died out of recollection by this time,—the conflict between the Archbishop of Cologne and the King of Prussia on the subject of mixed marriages. The Archbishop had refused to perform the marriage-ceremony between a Catholic and a Protestant in cases where there was not an agreement beforehand that the children should be brought up in the Catholic faith. For this sin against the law he had been imprisoned. To encourage and support him in his martyrdom Pope Gregory XVI. pronounced an allocution; and it is on this that the following glowing picture of Papal power and beneficent influence is founded. The writer begins by pointing out how complete an answer to all the reproaches of her enemies is the dignified protest against injustice thus made by Rome.

"Henceforward we shall be able to measure what point of downfall has been reached by that which is called a decrepit power, condemned to reign only over ruins. For us faithful Catholics, whom divine mercy has preserved from such fatal errors, we ought not less to thank the Vicar of our God for having so gloriously confounded his enemies, and for having thus deprived wandering yet believing souls of every excuse for their wandering. Let us await with humble admiration the day on which the light and transparent veil, which hid from us the long-suffering of our father, shall have been torn asunder. The glorious mystery of his justice has been all at once lighted by a great light. All at once we have been allowed to see how much force and energy there was in that patience which it is so hard to understand, but so glorious to possess, in an age so hungry of living, so eager for strife as ours; patience which passes the limits of human wisdom because it knows only those of divine charity, but patience which never goes so far as to give up a right or deny a truth. Yes, let us repeat it without ceasing, the Church is patient because she is immortal. But there comes a moment when she draws from her immortality a courage and strength, the mere shadow of which soars above all the strength and courage of this earth. All the Catholics who suffer, who groan under the yoke of heresy or persecuting schism, know now, that the moment will come when a sovereign balm will be dropped into the wounds of their hearts, and when, after rendering to Cæsar the things that are Cæsar's, they will hear a voice, which has echoed through eighteen centuries, bidding Cæsar render in his turn to God the things which are God's.

" . . . In the magnificent language of the Church, there is I know not what treasure of greatness and moderation, which transports the Christian soul with joy. She strikes without wounding, she sends forth her thunder without driving any to despair; and scarcely has she struck, scarcely has she thundered, when she stretches out her hand to heal and to raise up. Tell us, then, what power in the world could play the same part? Tell us what modern theory of society or of human government could produce a position like that of Rome? Tell us, in short, where is the power which could thus encamp, like an everlasting guardian, upon the threshold of the human conscience to keep it inviolable? And who else has the right and the will to say to people as to kings, to despotism as to anarchy, Hitherto shalt thou come, and no further?"

Nothing could give a better idea of the mind obstinately faithful to one belief, and inaccessible to any reasoning, so far as that was concerned, on one side—while at the same time open as day to actual experience of fact on the other. Never was man more tolerant in principle than Montalembert. The rights he claimed for himself he was ready and willing to accord to every Protestant; and we do not believe that any inducement would have persuaded him to wrong an individual heretic, or deprive him or her of any natural right, even for the advantage of the Church, much less his own. Yet in certain points his sight was obscured, or rather it was so firmly fixed in another direction that the opposite view escaped him, though it was one which in any other circumstances would have been the first to catch his eye. It is quite evident that in this business of the Cologne archbishop, the injustice of compelling a Protestant father or mother to relinquish all religious rights over their children, never occurred to him. His mind was entirely possessed by the spectacle of the "deux grands vieillards, l'un sur les bordes du Rhin, l'autre sur ceux du Tibre," "one dragged captive in the midst of bayonets and cannons with the match alight, because he would not profane a blessing—the other raising from the depths of his old palace a voice which does not perhaps command ten thousand soldiers, but which moves ten million souls;" and in sight of this great spectacle of the resistance of the spiritual to the secular, the much smaller apparitions of the Protestant bride or bride-groom, condemned to sacrifice for the sake of that blessing all claim upon his or her posterity,* steals away into the shadow and eludes his dazzled eyes. This, to our own thinking, is by much the most curious instance which has yet occurred in his history, of the paradoxical con-junction of tolerance and intolerance—profound regard for the rights of others, and absolute in-difference to them—devotion to liberty and sub-mission to authority—which characterised Mon-talembert. In everything else up to this point we are able to understand his rule of action, and to a certain extent to agree in it as prac-ticable and possible to a mind entirely loyal, honest, and true. But here we lose our chart,

* It is just to note, however, the Roman Catholic argument which is supposed to cover this natural injustice. It is that, while a Roman Catholic must almost despair of the salvation of his child's soul, which, cut of the Church, can be saved only by "invincible ignorance," the Protestant parent, who has no such fear, and who believes that a true believer in Christ will be saved in any communion, is in a much less painful position ; and that the sacrifice of the latter is only for this world, while on the part of the former it may be for eternity.

our clue through the labyrinth, and are compelled to fall back upon that old principle—old,
yet one of the newest in our modern code, and
which has nowhere been more faithfully held
than in England—that we have a right to take
away from those who disagree with us all facilities for spreading error, or even for bringing
up their successors in their own damnable
doctrines. Of itself this is a perfectly comprehensible theory, whether applied to problematical German babies or to the real hordes of
Irish infancy. The strange thing is to find it
along with all manner of generous, noble, and
tolerant thoughts in the mind of Montalembert.

In the year 1836 was published the Life of
Saint Elizabeth. This great era in a young
author's life, the publication of his first book, is,
however, eclipsed in that of Montalembert by
the much greater event which was close at
hand, and which already threw a rosy shadow
before. The work itself is one of which no
critic of the present day needs to speak. Of all
the saintly studies that have followed it, and
they have been many, none has successfully
emulated the beauty, the grace, the harmonious
charm of this beautiful book. The story itself
is so pure and sweet, so rich in poetry, so
tragic, yet so full of that angelic elevation

and tenderness which charm the pain away, that even under less skilful treatment it could scarcely fail to attract the general heart. But never was a hand more calculated to enhance all the lights of the picture than that of Montalembert. The simplicity and fulness of his own faith interpreted to him the self-devotion of his heroine ; and the stirrings of his own heart, the vague longing for love and companionship which had rent his young spirit during his first acquaintance with St Elizabeth, made him enter into the touching romance of her love with double sympathy. The book has all the charm of a love-story, of the tenderest and most ideal of romances, and of a saint's legend, in one. Nothing could be sweeter than the delightful childhood of the young Elizabeth, half angel, half baby, which opens up to us the whole old world in its quaint costume and wondrous ways ; unless, indeed, it were the pictures which we find a little further on, of the mediæval maiden in her absolute faith, full of a thousand sweet womanish excuses for her own virtue; and of the young wife clinging to her Crusader with that passion of love, and grief, and pride, and approval which inspires a woman and makes her heroic in her own despite. The young writer's whole heart was poured forth in this book. It was the first full revelation he had been able to make at once of himself, and of the ideal loftier than himself which possessed him. All his wanderings alone in the world, his longings for love and happier life, his readiness to sacrifice himself for his faith, his yearning over the lost and perishing, took shape in this life of visionary love, of heroic self-sacrifice, of submission and suffering and spiritual victory. La chère Sainte Elizabeth! The picture here presented was a portrait of her in the first place, a beautiful star of perfection, shining in the soft twilight sky of distant ages, drawing her biographer onward and upward—young, impassioned, capable of all griefs and delights as he was; and in another point of view it was an ideal picture of his own mind, expressing his thoughts and wishes and infinite endless musings, as in his own person he never could have done. With this stamp of reality upon it, in addition to all its poetical beauty and truth, no wonder that the book found great and instant favour. It is the very blossom and essence of Montalembert's life.

The work was preceded by a fine sketch of the history and character of the thirteenth century, showing much of the broader historical power which the author afterwards exhibited. It was dedicated to the gentle memory of his young sister — his own Elizabeth. Thus, not like a common book, but like the visionary, poetic revelation it was, it came into the world robed and adorned with the tender recollections of the past, and the undefined, passionate, youthful hopes of the future. We have seen a little case with two miniatures, which it was Montalembert's custom till the end of his life to carry about with him wherever he went, the portraits of two girlish faces : one over which her early fate has thrown to the spectator a gentle sadness ; the other fair and vigorous with the beauty of vitality. The two portraits are those of his sister and his bride. These two fair faces come before us as by magic when we take up the beautiful book which embodies and expounds the young writer's very heart; they hold it between them, the one inspiring him out of the celestial past into which she had gone, the other equally inspiring him out of the celestial unknown in which she still was. This was his poem which he chanted with his heart rent asunder by exquisite past sorrow which was not all pain, and inspired by the thrill of that unknown happiness which was to come.

CHAPTER X.

MARRIAGE.

OF the next great event in Montalembert's life we are grieved that we are not permitted to speak as the extreme beauty of the story would have tempted us to do. The reserve and natural delicacy of individual feeling close our lips upon one of the most exquisite, tender, pure, and touching of love-tales. It seems almost unnecessary to say that the ordinary French usages in respect to marriage were highly uncongenial to such a mind as his. The negotiations and family arrangements which are so common on the other side of the Channel, revolted him. He, who was full of the highest poetic "love of love," and appreciation of everything that is most beautiful and noble in the union of two hearts and spirits, had little patience or tolerance for the half - commercial transaction — so much *dot*, so many titles, social distinctions, or other compensating qualities—which takes the place in France of our more spontaneous though equally imperfect system. At this period of his life, as has been already recorded, he had been very deeply tantalised and rendered melancholy by the happy marriages of his two friends, Albert de la Ferronays and M. Rio. He had felt that the very sight of lovers and the name of love, gave him—so far was he from having part or lot in the matter—exquisite pain; and altogether his mind was in a very pensive mood. Lacordaire, too, had added to his discouragement even while he advised him to marry, by telling him that romances were rare in France, and that what St Teresa had said of her own time was true of this—" They love not." But if ever man was determined to make head against the custom of his time and country in any unworthy particular, that man was Montalembert; and Providence had reserved something better for him, a happiness as perfect and pure, an idyl as complete as that of Albert and Alexandrine. This idyl, we repeat, it is not for us to tell; nor can we dwell upon the happy ways, always and evidently providential in the eyes of bridegroom and bride, by which the new pair were brought together. He was married in August 1836 to a daughter of the noble house of De

Merode, one of the noblest in Belgium, and possessing also large estates in France—a family distinguished not only for pure and long descent, but for the most liberal and enlightened political principles, and which had taken a large share in the Revolution which made Belgium an independent kingdom. Madame de Montalembert was the daughter of Count Felix de Merode, already referred to, and the sister of the now well-known Monsignor de Merode, of whom all the world has heard. Their first meeting took place in the early spring of 1836, very shortly before the death of Albert de la Ferronays, which happened in Paris just at the moment when his friend had attained the crowning blessedness of life. The two scenes thus going on side by side were sadly different. Montalembert was one of the small circle assembled at that midnight mass in the dying man's chamber, where Alexandrine proclaimed herself a Catholic and received the communion along with her husband —a moment of mingled anguish and joy. This happened on the 3d of June: on the 29th, Albert died; and a fortnight later the Count and Countess de Merode, accompanied by their daughter, came to Paris to settle the preliminaries of the marriage. Thus the threads of life twine themselves together, the bitter and

the sweet, the infinitudes of youthful happiness
with those blacknesses of despair which cannot
be described in words. It was not despair that
followed Albert's death ; but a most Christian,
most submissive and holy sorrow. Yet, notwithstanding, there is always something heart-
rending in the mere vicinity of the widow and
the bride.

Immediately after their marriage, Montalembert and his young wife went at once by way
of Switzerland to Italy. In November we find
them at Venice, then in Rome, where they
passed the season of Christmas. The happy
lovers made a tender pilgrimage to those sacred
places where the other happy pair, who had
preceded them, and who were now separated by
death, had spent their early days. They went
to the room where Albert had suffered so much
in Venice, and murmured the *De profundis*
with low voices and swelling hearts. They
went and gazed at the Casa Margherita, where
Albert and Alexandrine had first met, and where
Montalembert had become the witness and confidant of their growing affection, but did not
enter the house, as it was " gorged with English."
Albert, indeed, as was natural, was very much
in their thoughts. " I fear to be ungrateful to
his holy memory," the happy bridegroom wrote

to Albert's young widow. "I fear to forget, in the midst of my new happiness, the ardent prayers and tender solicitude of him who, as you say, procured that happiness for me. And yet God knows that I constantly throw back my heart and thoughts upon Albert when I can detach them from the present. I have taken pleasure in feeling myself under the protection of him who was the closest companion of my life and the confidant of all my emotions, and who would have given, I am sure, a part of his happiness to preserve mine." There were many things throughout this journey which recalled the past, the recent past of 1832, with all its wanderings, to Montalembert—a recollection bitter in some points, very sad in others, but still not without its consolation ; for the one friend who remained of those who then shared his life, the Abbé Lacordaire, was again with him, meditating a step scarcely less important than that which the young Count had taken. Lacordaire was on the eve of entering the order of S. Dominic, a proceeding which may be said to have caused a sort of resurrection of the monastic orders, at least in France. In the mean time, however, he was once more the partaker of his friend's brightened existence, living in the same intimate and constant communion with him as they had enjoyed of old.

The young pair left Italy in March, the snow beating upon them as they left that country of flowers and sunshine; and in May we find Montalembert once more in Paris, and in his place in Parliament, where he spoke twice—once on the Emancipation of Slaves, and again upon the question of Ecclesiastical Property, the Government having proposed to take possession of the site of the ancient palace of the Archbishop of Paris, which had been sacked and almost destroyed in 1831, to make of it a public promenade. Montalembert spoke strongly and warmly, as might be looked for, against this project, but began his speech by expressing "loudly and without reserve" his admiration "for the two great acts by which, in the short space of one week, the Government has had the happiness and glory of distinguishing its policy." These two acts were —a general amnesty to prisoners condemned for political offences, and the restoration and reopening of the Church of St Germain l'Auxerrois; events of a very different character, yet both equally satisfactory to the champion of religion and of freedom.

The month of May, which was spent in Paris, supplies many touching scenes to the faithful journal which has preserved through all these years in the fragrance of its first freshness the happiest episode of its writer's life. May is the month of Mary; and there is a tenderness and effusion in the many services performed at the flower-decked altars, in which human feeling and all the sweetness of grateful recollection come in, making them to the devout Catholic a combination—perhaps not very comprehensible to many of us—of divine worship and tender personal celebration of the merits of a real human friend, which is very exquisite in its appeal to the feelings. Perhaps no Protestant will ever really be able to seize the infinite shades of difference between the worship of adoration which the Roman Catholic Church, like all others, reserves for God alone, and the worship of veneration which she so lavishly extends to His saints, and, above all, to the Virgin. Yet that there is a difference, and that the one kind of religious service is carefully discriminated—at all events in the minds of all intelligent worshippers—from the other, is a fact which few who have taken the trouble to study the question from a non-polemical point of view will dispute. The confusion of the heretic understanding, when it attempts to fathom this fine and delicate difference, is not perhaps shared by the faithful believer, who has been trained all his life to look up to Mary as to another and more elevated mother. But young Montalembert and his young wife, when they set out together in those early summer evenings in the delightful independence and companionship of their new life, might well attract all the sympathy of the looker-on, whatever were his opinions. They went now to one church, now to another, enjoying the tender religious sentiment, and the overwhelming sense of their own happiness; and then would walk home together in the soft May moonlight, surrounded by an atmosphere of blessedness, finding everything lovely, fragrant, melodious. Paris itself, which has seen so many strange and terrible scenes, grows hushed and peaceful about these two young figures; the river flows softly, the towers of Nôtre Dame rise with a protecting grace against the background of softened blue; and under the dark arches of St Eustache, where they betake themselves sometimes from the stillness of their noble quarter across the river, how the lights shine on the white-decked altar, and the *Salve Regina* rises on delicious voices into the great darkness of the vaulted roof! That music rose straight to heaven while those young hearers listened to it in simple and unquestioning devotion; and heaven itself was with them in this soft, genial, religious May.

The only grief which Montalembert records at this moment is one which the reader will not feel to be very serious. He was deeply distressed that his wife would not admire a certain church, of which we have unfortunately forgotten the name! He could not bear that there should be even this point of difference. At the same time, however, while he gravely records this lover-like distress, he was not so much absorbed or rapt in his new bliss as to be indifferent to the events which were going on, or to give up the occupations of his life. A long and most careful analysis of Rio's book on Christian Art, the first worthy recognition which it had received, dates from this early summer; and he even congratulates himself in his journal that his happiness does not disqualify him from interest and action in other matters.

The rest of the summer was spent at Villersexel, a vast and interesting old chateau belonging to the family of Madame de Montalembert, one of the many noble houses which has been destroyed by Prussian guns during the recent war. Here Montalembert's enthusiasm for architectural beauty was fully satisfied. We are not aware whether it was at this moment, or at an earlier period, that, while examining the genealogical records of the family of which he now formed a part, he made the delightful discovery that the beautiful young wife whom he adored was of the very blood and lineage of his dear St Elizabeth! a discovery which made him more and more gratefully conscious of the benediction of Heaven upon him in his happy union. Here, too, was born his eldest child, christened Elizabeth-Hiltrude, the second name being that of the saint whose little chapel stood in the ancestral woods, and whose holy well was the object of many pilgrimages. In this well the ring of betrothal had been dipped which first united the pair; and now their child was placed under the protection of this woodland patroness, as well as of the loftier and more renowned saint, who was at once her mother's ancestress and the heavenly lady of her father's knightly devotion. Such delightful prejudices of the heart have no place among our religious thoughts; yet how charming is the human grace with which they link the present to the past!

After this new beginning of life there followed a few years of tranquil domestic existence, not without movement and that *bruit* which, from his earliest days, Montalembert had acknowledged himself to love—but still calm, disturbed by no clamour of perpetual publicity, with time in it

for much literary work and much family enjoyment. The agitation which filled some years of
his later life with continual bustle and business,
that assault upon the monopoly of the University,
and claim for freedom of teaching, which had
so early occupied him, was taken up to a certain
extent during these gentle years, but not with
that determined tenacity of purpose which inspired him at a later period ; and in his leisure
the more congenial subject of Art came uppermost,
and suggested most of his literary themes. The
question of Freedom in Education was not yet
ripe for discussion. Since its old champions had
fallen under Papal censure, the question itself
had dropped, as it were, out of fashion. It had
become entangled in the ruins of the ' Avenir,'
and none had dared to disinter it, or assume
to themselves any share of the opprobrium
which had crushed and quenched that im-
prudent pioneer of freedom ; and a host of
difficulties were involved in its resuscitation.
The bishops of France looked coldly on it, and
indeed upon all enterprises which required agitation. " Le bruit ne fait jamais de bien, et le
bien ne fait jamais de bruit," said one of them,
with epigrammatic wisdom ; and probably this
mot itself did much to prevent the possibility
of organising any constitutional agitation on

this important subject. Foiled, therefore, for the moment in the special object which he pursued without failing or forgetfulness for so many years, Montalembert turned, as we have said, to Art, the other subject which attracted him most. In 1837 his paper on the "État actuel de l'art religieux en France" was published. His sketch, "Du Vandalisme," had appeared only four years before, and already he was able to speak of improvement and progress such as he had not hoped for.

"An immense change," he says, "has been worked in men's minds since the time when we were moved to raise a humble, unknown, and almost solitary voice against the Vandals of various kinds who were devastating the monuments of our faith and our history. In a very few years the aspect of affairs has changed. The Revolution of July, while it gave the last blow to the *ancien régime*, in the present and in the future, gave a new impulse to the study and understanding of the *ancienne France* in the past—not the bastard and inconsistent past of recent centuries, but the past of that great period when Christianity reigned over humanity, soul and body. The new Government placed itself frankly on the side of the party, very few in number, which, moved by the invectives of M. Victor Hugo, attempted to struggle against the torrent of destruction. Using their power with salutary energy, M. Guizot and his successors, as Minister of the Interior and as Minister of Public Instruction, have extended the immense and inevitable arms of civilisation to arrest the municipal hammer and the industrial brush, while at the same time they have instituted and encouraged vast and important publications, the object of which was to raise the treasures of national art from the dust, and to reveal them to the country. This noble and excellent example ought to have been given by Government at an earlier period, and will, thank God, be necessary in the future. On the other hand, a deeper study of foreign countries has produced unexpected results. On examining more closely the habits and the learning of England and Germany, men have learnt to understand the profound respect and tender care professed by these great nations for the monuments of their past ; and, turning their thoughts back on their own country, they have found out with surprise and admiration that France still possesses in her provincial towns, notwithstanding the melancholy nakedness of some and the ridiculous decoration of others, cathedrals more beautiful than the most celebrated in England.

Among the dust of her libraries have been found poems more original and full of inspiration than the most popular epics of Germany; and the manuscripts of these poems have been found to be adorned by miniatures more exquisite and delicate than even the much-vaunted miniatures of the Vatican. Thus the world has at last found out and understood that even in France there exists another kind of art, another kind of beauty, than the material beauty and pagan art of the times of Louis XIV. and of the Empire."

Of this change Montalembert himself was one of the chief originators; and though he goes on to complain that "unfortunately this discovery has been made chiefly by literary men or travellers," yet there can be little doubt that he felt the creation of the Committee of Historical Art, in 1834, and that of the Commission on Historical Monuments, which was brought into being in this very year 1837, to be partly his own doing. Of both of these committees he was subsequently appointed a member, and continued to work actively upon them until the days of the Empire, at which time, as is succinctly and significantly stated in a note to his article on Religious Art, " He was excluded from the *Comité des Arts* by an order signed Fortoul, and dated September 14, 1852; and from the *Commission des*

Monuments Historiques by an imperial decree of the 15th December 1860, countersigned A. Walewski." The Empire was no more favourable to his severe and pure conceptions of Christian art, than to others of his most cherished opinions.

The article on "l'Etat actuel de l'art religieux " was chiefly directed against the debased sentiment of pictures and sculptures professing to be religious; and was followed by a second article, " De l'attitude actuelle du Vandalisme en France," in which the writer castigates with merciless precision the general mass of Frenchmen, who, notwithstanding all the remonstrances of antiquarians and the efforts of Government, still persisted in regarding old churches and convents as so many immense quarries for the reparation of their own houses, or aid of their own funds. We might add a long list of speeches and of shorter writings, all with the same end and meaning. The *laideur systématique* of public buildings, the vile taste of the decorations with which the Peers were surrounded in the Luxembourg, the levity of the music often heard in churches—all attracted his notice and criticism in their turn. Few people out of France, and perhaps only a limited number even there, are aware of his unwearying labours in this department of the public service.

"In the end of 1838 Montalembert appeared as the champion of Belgium, then threatened with the loss of the Duchy of Luxembourg, which was accomplished at a later period. This speech is a very fine and eloquent protest against those interferences with popular rights and partitions of kingdoms which were so summary and so general after the great wars of the beginning of the century; and at the same time against that tyrannical interposition in the affairs of a small State which Europe has always permitted to herself, in compensation for her want of courage in interfering with the greater. It is unnecessary for us to enter into this long-ended argument; but there are many things in the speech which return upon the reader's ear with a strange echo after all the events of the late few years, which, happily for himself, Montalembert did not live to see. When he protests eloquently against the change of allegiance proposed, demanding " from the height of this tribune so much delay as may suffice to consult the wishes of the people, the wishes of three hundred thousand souls, who are your brothers, your neighbours, who, in one word, are men, and have a right to be otherwise treated than thus to be bartered and sold like cattle; " when he trembles for the effect which may be produced, " in our eastern provinces, upon the patriotic population of Lorraine and Alsace by that army assembled on their frontier, by the sight of their neighbours, their brothers, delivered up to Prussian bayonets;"—what strange, confused, half-prophetic sentiment of the future breathes through the words which are now so much more sadly and painfully significant! The whole discussion trembles with unforeseen issues; no one of all these men, wise in their statesmanship, but short-sighted by reason of their humanity, had any insight into that future which lies so darkly before us. "Do not imagine," cries the generous defender of all oppressed countries, "that I sigh for war, for conquest, for the extension of our borders, for the frontier of the Rhine. No; I declare loudly I desire for my country neither war nor conquest, nor the addition of a single village, of a single inch of territory; but there are other victories, moral conquests—and it is these which I desire for my country. I wish it to be known everywhere on our frontiers, in every cabin, that France is a peaceful neighbour, faithful to every pledge, the friend of justice, of true freedom, of genuine order, ready to maintain these against all comers, and under whose protection the humblest may rest in peace. These are the only conquests which I desire."

It is curious, too, to note the different aspect

under which Belgium and her affairs then appeared to the mind of Europe. We of this later generation have been trained in the belief that England is the natural protector of that prudent and sensible little country; and indeed, the possible invasion or partition of Belgium has become almost the only question which kindles in their ashes something of our ancient fires; but forty years ago this would not seem to have been so. The Government of July felt itself almost the parent of the nation which had secured its independent being by a revolution immediately following that of France. "How can the interest of England in Belgium be for a moment compared to ours?" asks Montalembert. "The interest of England is to maintain the kingdom of the Netherlands, for that was her erection—it is her favourite work; and certainly to take any step in another direction was an immense concession on her part to the French alliance. Is there between her and Belgium, as between Belgium and us, identity of revolution, or of language, or of customs, or of religion? Nothing of the kind. England may have given up Belgium, but is that a reason why we in our turn should give her up?"

This throws a curious light upon the position of the nations. King Leopold was the son-in-law of the French king, and France no doubt had a great many more reasons to be interested in her little but useful neighbour than we could have. But nothing can more clearly show how far the France of the Empire was separated from the France of the house of Orleans than this discussion, read in the light of that famous Secret Treaty against the independence of Belgium, which to our English understandings almost read like an assault upon ourselves.

In the year 1839 Montalembert paid a short and melancholy visit to England, to the death-bed of his mother; a visit of which few traces are to be found. He appeared at a meeting of the Friends of Poland held in London on the 15th of June, at which the Duke of Sussex was in the chair, and where in a short and somewhat embarrassed speech (for was it not his habit, and that of all France, to speak of Ireland as another Poland ?) he recommended the cause of the Poles to English sympathy, describing it as one of the chief bonds between our country and his, " the best guarantee of the alliance between France and England;" and picturing to his hearers " the two first nations of the world " marching to the succour of that oppressed nationality, with the words of " the inspired poet of Ireland " on their lips—

> " The friends we've tried are by us,
> And the foe we hate before us."

On this visit Montalembert was accompanied by his wife and brother-in-law, Count Werner de Merode, but the melancholy occasion of it prevented them from entering into society in London; the only exceptions they made, as M. Rio informs us, being in favour of "a young member of Parliament, destined to the greatest political position of our time"—to wit, Mr Gladstone; and old Samuel Rogers, then one of the most notable personages in society. The effect produced upon this veteran by the visit of the Catholic enthusiast was of a curious kind, and one does not know whether to smile or to be touched by M. Rio's *naïve* account of his old friend's emotion, and the cause he assigned for it.

"When I found myself alone with Rogers (after the departure of Montalembert and his party), the expression of his countenance, which up to that moment had been smiling and animated, changed so suddenly that I feared I had offended him by some word of doubtful meaning which I might not altogether have understood. He paced about the room without saying anything, and I did not know whether I might venture to break this incomprehensible silence. At last he broke it himself, and then I understood that our recent conversation and the sight

of the young pair so perfectly happy in the
unanimity of their faith had touched a chord
which vibrated to the depths of his being. When
I returned home I wrote the following words in
my journal on this subject : ' After the three
others had gone, Rogers said to me that if he
had the power of putting himself in the place of
another, he would choose that of Montalembert,
not on account of his youth and his beautiful
wife, but because he possessed that immovable
and cloudless faith which seemed to himself the
most enviable of all gifts.' "

This is not the aspect under which we are
accustomed to consider the man who was so
long a kind of grandfather of English literature,
though his own claims to poetic fame are of so
mild a nature ; but probably it represents a side
of his character which he did not reveal to the
common eye.

END OF THE FIRST VOLUME.

PRINTED BY WILLIAM BLACKWOOD AND SONS, EDINBURGH.

In Five Volumes 8vo, price £2, 12s. 6d.,

THE MONKS OF THE WEST,

FROM ST BENEDICT TO ST BERNARD.

BY

THE COUNT DE MONTALEMBERT.

TRANSLATED BY MRS OLIPHANT.

CONTENTS.

- - - - - - - - - -

WILLIAM BLACKWOOD & SONS, EDINBURGH AND LONDON.